I0190298

Comeback Power

Recovery

(C.P.R.)

Self Recovery
from
alcohol, drugs
and
negative behaviors.

One decision at a time

A true gift of love and hope
for those seeking positive life change.

Michael K. Hensley, B.A.

Comeback Power Recovery

Contact author for orders, comments etc.

www.comebackpowerrecovery.com
www.substanceabuserecovery.web.officelive.com

comebackpowerrecovery@live.com
emailmike2003@yahoo.com

First edition
First Printing January 2010

Published in Waterford Michigan
The United States of America

ISBN# 978-0-615-33910-8

© 2009 Michael K. Hensley
All Rights Reserved

Library of Congress Control Number 2009912781

No part of this book may be reproduced or transmitted in any form or any means, including photocopy, recording or storage and retrieval system, without author's written permission.

Disclaimer: Comeback Power Recovery (C.P.R.) is a personal self help guide, to be used individually, or to supplement other helping programs. It is to help raise awareness of the importance of personal decisions, responsibility and self talk in breaking the bondages of learned and addictive behaviors.

C.P.R. is not a medical supplement and should not be treated as such. Dependency and addiction are serious conditions which should be treated under the guidance of a qualified physician who can help with the often dangerous withdrawal symptoms associated with dependency and addiction.

C.P.R.

Eliminating negative thinking and behaviors

C.P.R has been created to be used by and for the individual, yet is compatible with and may be used in starting, or supplementing, other helping groups or programs. It can be used as is, as an individual standalone life change program, to help implement changes in personal thinking processes and behaviors, or may be modified to fit the needs and goals of any changing person, group or program.

C.P.R. understands the need for citizen's, communities and programs to be willing and capable of working together to bring the best chances to the person, as C.P.R. knows that the individual is the most important part of the equation and must be taught that in order to change life, one must learn to change past thinking and behaviors and to accept and implement these positive productive changes in the now.

If your life seems lost or empty and if you are actively using alcohol or drugs remember that you are not looking to function with a problem, you are working to eliminate the problem and by realizing this, your victorious journey has begun. Now is the time to stand up and learn to be proud of yourself for who you are becoming, as you make the decision to change and you will change and will keep changing, one decision at a time, as you learn to live beyond your feelings and others opinions and to stand by your new positive life truths, until your life becomes a sea of good decisions.

Now is the time for you to prepare to find the life that you have been seeking and C.P.R. is going to walk with you, as you find the good that is waiting to spring forth in your new thinking and your new life. Remember as you move through C.P.R. that you have nothing to lose and everything good, about you and life, to gain, also be advised that this is the unedited edition and I am no English professor, so please go easy on policing any minor grammatical errors, as I am a person, just like you.

Forward:

When seeking to change negative life behaviors, such as ending addiction thinking, the individual needs a plan and path for finding and building on the personal responsibilities, strengths and life goals needed to effectively achieve productive self recovery. C.P.R. will help in this life change, as the individual works towards recovery, through the hourly repetition of good positive thoughts and productive decision making skills, while also working to eliminate any negative thoughts and behaviors that have been hindering one's own chance at "the good life". C.P.R. will work with, guide and strengthen the individual while teaching how to achieve recovery in the now, as the objective of recovery is the building up of personal strengths, skills and responsibilities, through today's decision making efforts. Throughout C.P.R. you will find that positive, productive current life goals will guide the life change process and that this change will become possible, through hard work and believing in oneself, while taking a firm hold of one's life changing recovery decisions.

The individual now has a viable chance at full recovery through responsible decision making, while realizing that past decisions hold no bearing on the power of good decision making in the now. The individual will be changing thoughts, behaviors and distorted ways of thinking away from yesterday's, oppressive, addiction thinking and towards a more powerful, self actualized, now thinking, as recovery is a decision by and for the individual and it is the individual that holds the keys to that decision.

It is time to see that the responsibility for your actions is yours and though alcohol and drugs may have affected your thought processes, you are responsible for your decisions and it is by these decisions that your life will be changed, one decision at a time.

With C.P.R. you will use your desire to change and your drive to do better, as you learn to eliminate the negative behaviors of addiction and the excuses that reinforce them; as this is a program of behavior, thought and life changes through finding and building on the personal inherent individual strengths and powers which you do possess.

Positive change through 10,000 positive thoughts a year

Life is not about being "the best person", it is about being "the best person that you can be, to yourself and for yourself, at this exact moment in time", which will come through good decision making in the now, as making a good decision is not a future event, it starts now, is something that you control now and is the only feasible way to deal with anything as dangerous as negative behaviors and addiction.

Now is the time to be looking forward and paying close attention to your next decisions, while doing the best that you can do with them, so that you will never have to waste time looking back thinking that you could have done better when you need to be looking forward and just doing better.

It is time to see how the repetition of thoughts will work to change your thinking, as good decisions are like a paycheck; you reap rewards for good work and good decisions alike and just like a job, when you get paid for one hour it may not do much, but when you put it together with 40 more, you can live a better life because of it. So think about making good decisions and saying many good positive things about yourself every hour of every day, which would give you a 168 positive hours and minimum of 168 positive thoughts per week, which is a reasonable and obtainable request of and for yourself and would be at least 800 positive thoughts per month going into your conscious and unconscious mind and that is looking in the right direction for brain retraining and life change.

Make sure to also think about this in the other direction; if you heard, saw, said or allowed more than one negative word, thoughts or action every hour, do you not believe that this many negative thoughts going into your mind would not affect your thinking, as they do add up, if you allow them in?

The good news is that all of the negatives can become a thing of the past, as you find a new way of thinking; and just like a used car, when you get a new one it would not make sense to drag the old one around behind you; so you get rid of it and forget about it, just as you will do with your past thinking and bad thoughts; exchange them for new and forget about them, as you now learn to enjoy your new ride and investment, through 10,000 positive thoughts a year.

Author's story (short version)

Everyone has a story of woe and wow, and at times we can learn from those who have walked the walk of pain and desperation and who have found the courage and wisdom to seek change. I have been there and have found that people have the capacity for change, no matter how deeply buried in these feelings of complete desperation that often accompany addiction. I had no idea how each of my own decisions was affecting my life; until I ended up an alcohol driven, panic stricken, compulsive drunk. I fell in deeper and deeper and eventually became tortured every minute of every day, as I fell inside addiction and the fears brought on through the brain changes from this poison. It was not long before I no longer new rational life; I had unconsciously traded for the irrational drinking thinking, as I battled alcohol abuse, panic attacks along with physical and mental health depletion, as I was robbed, beaten, dumped on, ridiculed and kicked out to the curb to die, for my bad decision making.

The devastation from addiction had engulfed my mind, body, spirit and soul. I had no idea what was happening in my life or mind, just that something was taking everything from me, including killing every hope, dream and vision that I ever had. The torment and pain was increasing and never ending, something had a stranglehold on my life and would not let go. I was stranded in a whirlwind of addiction and panic; watching my life disappear into a blur of confusion and desperation as I felt these forces ripping and tearing my mind and soul in half; one side would not let go and let me live, the other side would not let go to die; I felt that there was no hope, as I just wanted to die and this is what alcohol and drugs has to offer so many lives.

I was homeless, scared and trying to fit in, but nobody wants a scared, depressed, drunk hanging around and I became very sad, sick and lonely, battling addiction and panic disorder. I would find a place in the cold dark night to sit and shake and ride the panic train all night and then spend the new day preparing for another night of terror and freezing. I longed for a safe warm night's sleep and to believe for a moment that someone cared about me enough to wonder if I was dead or alive, hungry, or ?, I needed someone who cared that I was hurting so bad that I wanted to die.

One doctor helped; he told me I was going die. The alcohol was eating me alive and I had a lot of pain, damage and bleeding; my eyesight was failing, I had lost a lot of weight and was near crippled; in mind, body and spirit, I was having violent seizures, often waking up in the hospital, to be thrown back out in the streets once sober. On one trip they tried to admit me into a mental hospital, but found nothing wrong, outside of the addiction, which they no longer treated, so they too threw me back out in the streets. So here I was; a self proclaimed nobody, living in a state of walking death, where nobody wanted me; family and friends did not care to have me around, it did not seem like God wanted me, the hospitals and mental institutions did not want me, I surely did not want me, what else was there? The bottle wanted me, but it wanted me sick and dead of which it finally did achieve its goal, when I was in my twenties. I was found in the streets, in convulsions and my heart was stopping, the blood alcohol level had peaked and my behaviors finally had beaten me down and the alcohol was finally going to end another life, it was sad, but I did not know how to break these ties that alcohol held.

There was nothing in this world that could have saved me! Or was there? At the last minute I found that this oppression could be beat and no matter how far gone your life feels, it is time that you see that there is more than a chance for you and it starts with your next decision and goes on, one decision at a time. I too "felt" that there was nothing that I could do, but I was wrong, because anyone can live beyond what they feel and start making good decisions based on, "I can" regardless of the feeling, and this is where you learn how to live a life free from the excuses, fears and oppressions of addiction thinking.

So start making good decisions, even when it is hard and when you feel that you cannot do it, do it anyways and if you are afraid, then do it afraid, if you are alone do it alone. It is time to start listening to the person inside you that wants to hear what you can do; not those that tell you what you cannot do and you need to spend the rest of the days and nights thinking about every next productive good decision that you can make, for you and start making them, one at a time.

Beginning thoughts

Comeback Power Recovery is a personal, positive, productive, life enhancing, self-recovery program. C.P.R. can assist one in living a life free from the negative thoughts, behaviors and burdensome costly weights of past programming, brought on by the bad decision making and distorted thinking, as well as the faulty societal misconceptions associated with the negative behavioral conditioning of addiction. C.P.R. offers the individual a chance of self recovery and a new plan for a controlled now life, while emphasizing the importance of the positive, productive, inherent abilities of each person, as well as the importance of the personal choices, actions and responsibilities leading towards a secure a foundation of self-actualization.

It is time to better understand the decision making skills that you possess and which you will be using to help build your C.P.R. recovery life. You will find that though it is you that is doing this for yourself, that you are not doing it by yourself and you will need to learn to start working your interdependent role in the community as you come to understand the interactive norms of the social networks that pertain to you as an interdependent member of society. You can be assured that you will be gaining and not giving up power through these interdependencies, as it will take all of your good inherent powers to break these binds that have been hindering your life.

You are going to find that you harness much more of this needed power than you realize, which will become self evident, as you start using your personal C.P.R. decisions productively, which starts as a decision to end negative behaviors, to change bad thinking and to start living responsibly, as you move into victory over addiction through complete thinking and behavior changes.

This life change is a decision which has to be made by you, for you and about you, as no one except you, can force you to become a better person to or for yourself. Your recovery must be a personal decision to no longer reside in past thinking or addiction, as you cannot live in the past and thrive in the present at the same time and now is the time to decide on a new beginning, with a new hope, for a new and better now life, as you come to see that no matter how troubled your past or your present life feels, you have survived, maybe not unscathed, but more alive and stronger than you realize, due to your will, power and quest for a better life.

This is your personal victory that you are moving into and it is time to realize that the power that you possess over life, addiction and the past is the power of your decisions and now is the time for new decisions, about new life and now life, as life is now and it is meant to be lived in the now. It takes enough work to live for and to be happy for today, so stop dragging the past around and instead of wishing for a better yesterday and hoping for a better tomorrow, learn how to start working on your next good decisions, for a better now, today.

It is also time to realize that being liked by others is nice, but it is not a life sustaining necessity; where being loved by oneself is. So if you want change in your life, than you must start realizing that you are going to need to be open to new ideas, including learning to like and love yourself, because of the person that you are and that you are becoming.

C.P.R. is based on individual strengths, needs and desires, as well as personal experience, true knowledge, logical thinking and research and though it is not a substitute for professional medical services, it will promote an awareness of how to break the bonds of addiction, compulsive behaviors and bad decisions, through teaching individuals how to change destructive thinking habits, while also showing how to find a new hope for a productive life.

Be sure to read study and work the plans with each new day, as this is how life change works. Also be sure to welcome repetition as a positive learning tool, in retraining and socializing your mind, as your positive affirmations, productive actions and self talk will be strengthened through the repetition of good thoughts.

Do not just read the plans and expect them to work for you, as you must learn to work with them, read them and reread them and then work them and rework them, know them and understand them, as hearing the right things over and over will work to retrain your conscious and unconscious thinking and thought processes.

C.P.R. thoughts for the day

Today is the best day of my life;
Today is the day that I will control my decisions and I will bring about life change through my power to think and act differently and to make better decisions today than I made yesterday, because my new life is now.

Today I will work to achieve recovery and accomplish changes in my thinking, starting with my next decision and moving on; one decision at a time, until my life becomes a sea of good decisions.

Today I am willing to learn to live beyond my feelings, emotions and ego, as I come to a point of controlled emotions and feelings, with no ego satisfactions. I will get beyond feelings and thinking that I know best and start working on what is best and will not be afraid to admit that at times, I have made the wrong decisions and that is okay, as that is the past.

Today I will welcome positive change in my thinking, as I become willing to listen, to think, to learn and to change; as these are the keys to my vehicle of change and I will use them wisely, as I learn new things about myself and life and then this truly can be the best day of my life.

Today I am ready to put away the false knowledge and beliefs, which were learned through past distorted thinking, gossip and hearsay; as I am now ready to accept that many of the things that I once believed, may not be as true as I thought and I will start replacing these false beliefs with the factual truths that I will be using to walk through my new day and my new recovery life.

Today I will implement positive change in my life and will move into positive, productive recovery by working my C.P.R. plans, with open mindedness, a willingness to learn and a personal recovery attitude, as I know that life may never be easier, but through my positive productive decisions it will be better.

Comeback Power Recovery

Table of Contents:

1.0 Time for change

It is time to realize that whatever you think about the current condition of your life, that you are not "too far gone" to benefit from the positive life change that will come as a result of working through your C.P.R. life recovery plans. You do have the power of life change within your grasp if you will work for and accept it, while implementing the positive productive life changes needed for you to build a stronger and better recovery life for your today, one good decision at a time.

As with any life change program, you must be willing to grow and to hear things differently than you may be used to and you must be willing to start taking responsibility for and doing your full part in your recovery. You will start by paying closer attention to your responsibilities, decisions and self talk, as you quit making excuses for your past ways of thinking and living, because the past does not need excuses, it needs to be forgiven and forgotten, for good.

It is also time to stop hiding behind misinformation and to see that self-recovery and a better life is for all who are willing to work for it, including the first time or casual drinker, who mistakenly thinks that they can be responsible drinkers, or the 20 year compulsive drinker that knows better, too the foolish new drug experimenter trying to fit in to be cool, or the chronic addict trying to get out before they are cold, it is for those who are tired of old ways of thinking and who want to see change in their lives and those who are willing to learn and grow and realize that all people need and are capable of true life change.

If you drink, or use drugs, or entertain any other learned negative thoughts or behaviors than you need to realize that the decisions about your life that you made this morning, yesterday and over the years, has nothing to do with your next decision, your today, your recovery, or your life in the now.

So stop dragging bad decisions, bad thoughts and bad pasts around and letting them influence and oppress your good decisions. It is time to realize that the past is like an ice cube sitting in the desert; it disappears fast and is gone forever, now you can start digging for it, you can drag its memory around and can complain about it all day long, but it is not coming back, you cannot change it and it will never do anything more for you, so do not bury it to be dug up again later, learn from it, forgive it and throw it away, to melt away and be gone forever.

You must learn to make your next decisions wisely, regardless of the past, as you are now looking forwards, not backwards and you must let your past melt away within self forgiveness, as it is time to see that torturing yourself will not fix the past, nor help the now and is always wrong no matter how you falsely justify it.

So make amends for your past when feasible, but not at the expense of harming your now life, as now is the time to heal, forgive and stop dragging hard times around with you, as you do not have to wait until you cannot stand anymore pain to make the decision to change directions and to stand up and face what is ahead. True change becomes a matter of realizing that the mind thrives on what you feed it, so start feeding it well and it will do well, but keep feeding it poison and it will become poisoned.

So make the decision to eliminate poisonous thinking and stop reaffirming, "the bad days", bad thoughts and bad feelings, while wondering why you cannot get feeling better; because bad days are created, they do not just happen; though bad moments and bad decisions may, but dragging them around, or dragging yourself through them, will not help your day or life get better. Walk through them with the right attitude, change them if you can, dispose of them as you must and move on with your new day, which starts right now.

Remember to continue your positive productive self-talk, as you cannot start a new day reinforcing negative thoughts and feelings and then expect the day to be a positive event, but you can take control of it and feel good through your own thought processes and decisions, so start changing your thought processes and choosing your words and attitudes carefully, as it is time to start making conscious decisions about taking control of your present life conditions and realizing that your next decisions are the life decisions that will affect your now life and continuing recovery in the now.

(Day 1) **1.1 Erasing old programming**

It is time for you to start using your ability to think more effectively, while eliminating the negative oppressive thinking that has kept you from becoming the person that you are capable of becoming. As you start your journey and prepare for self-recovery, through learning to eliminate negative thinking and behaviors, you are going to realize that much of life is lived in your thoughts and that no matter where your life seems to be heading, there is a better place within your reach, even if it has become hidden in the thoughts that you have been entertaining through the life that you have been enduring.

You will find your new self recovery to be like a seed, buried underneath a ton of dark oppressive dirt and yet patiently waiting for the chance to spring forth and stand tall, with new chances at new life, to stand above that which held it down for so long. There will be battles along the way, but by staying moving in the right direction, just like that seed, you will shake off this oppressive dirt and grow stronger every day.

So keep striving for change through the powers of your decisions, as now is the time to become responsible and to move away from the addictive thinking that has buried your mind under this ton of oppressive pity party dirt. It is time to see that you cannot wait until tomorrow to do better today, as you must learn to live and grow in the now, while remembering that mistakes and all that you are deserving of a life free from addiction and negative behaviors and that it will be through your hard work and your decisions that you will find this new life.

This change that you seek will come through brain retraining, recognizing negative thought patterns and eliminating the false knowledge that has been holding your mind captive for so long. You will be standing on new truths and will find that it is not only okay to talk to yourself, but that it is a skill which needs perfected, while being mindful of what you are saying, as your brain will believe, feel, or use whatever you teach it, which includes not just the positive affirmations and uplifting thoughts that you need to guide you towards victory, but also all the negative words, attitudes, actions, thoughts and persecutions that you speak, hear, see and continuously allow into your life and mind.

You must not waste any more time on these negative thoughts and behaviors, as it is time to erase the bad programming that has engulfed your confidence and imprisoned your true powers of recovery and to wipe the slate clean of past bad decisions and make room for new positive learning, as you start reclaiming control of your life, thoughts and behaviors through Comeback Power.

You will come to see that though alcohol can affect your thinking, it is still under your will, your power and your decisions that you operate and you can spend a lifetime lying to yourself and blaming everything else for your actions, but to learn to live life positively you must become honest and take responsibility for life and then and only then will you find your true powers working for you, as you find that it is you that exerts the power and makes the final decisions for your actions.

So now it is time to own up to your life decisions and reactions for all that they are, bad behaviors, from bad decisions and to realize that these behaviors are learned and as such, they can be unlearned, through changing your daily input and output, by becoming mindful of your self-talk (input), as well as of your life decision and attitudes (output).

You must realize that you have the right to make good decisions and to tell your brain good things about yourself and then you must make a commitment to start replacing all your negative talk and behaviors, with positive thoughts and actions. Remember that your mind only knows what you teach it and only acts on what you tell it, so if you teach yourself to get mad every time a leaf falls off a tree, in time that is exactly what will happen. Now teach your mind that life is good, even with its trials and tribulations and in time you will see that life can be good where it matters the most, in your thoughts, your mind and your decisions.

So be honest with yourself, control your thoughts and work through the C.P.R. plans to discover who you are and who you truly can be, as well as what you truly believe and what you can do to make your life a positive productive event, one plan and one decision at a time, because you and your life are worth all of your efforts.

(Day 1b) **1.1 #1 study thought. Erasing old programming**

It is time to stop viewing people and life in terms of "good or bad" as you must learn to separate them from the deeds and events and realize that all people are capable of and deserve positive change, including you, but you must be ready and willing to change your thinking and to accept life change.

How would you answer the following;
I believe that I am a _____ person? Why do you believe this?

Be sure to think of yourself in terms of "a person" and not by the deeds that you have done, as you are not a good or bad person; you are "a person", who has done some good or bad deeds, as we all have, but these are not who or what you are?

What do you honestly know or believe about yourself? Why?
What do others know or believe about you? How and Why?

Do you the difference in believing, or knowing something?
Do you know why beliefs do not equal truths? Why?

Do you know, or believe, that you are capable of change? Why?
Are you willing to accept changes in your beliefs? Why?
What kind of changes in your thinking, thoughts, behaviors and life are you willing to accept? Why? How?

What do you need for you to decide to start changing?
I could do better if (or by) _____? If what? By what?
Could you stop the excuses and start doing better, just because of your decision to do better? How? When?

What is stopping you from doing all that you can do to become a better person to yourself? How can you change this?
I am willing to work on becoming a _____person by doing___?
By doing what? What can you start doing right now to start becoming the person that you want to become?

Do you want to change how others feel about you? Why? How could you accomplish this? Will it help your recovery?

Remember that it is more important what you know and feel about yourself than what others believe about you!

What do you know about the thoughts, moods and attitudes that you take in and carry with you throughout your day?
How many negative, thoughts, words, feelings "just words", "don't mean a thing", I can not's, do not, should not, could not, did not's, do you ingest every day? What about hearsay, gossip, complaining, vulgar words and pity thoughts e.g. nobody cares, I'm no good, I could have, never could, why me, why not me, what about me, whatever, I don't care, not my problem, I'm depressed, life's not fair, it sucks, the worlds against me; plus all those used in jest or quick temperedness e.g. that was stupid, I can be so dumb, what is wrong with me and all the trash talk taken in from negative people, television, radio, music, magazines and all the places that breed negativity, bad attitudes, drinking thinking etc.

So again, how many negatives do you allow into your mind and how do you think that they affect your life chances? As there are no just words, they are all thoughts that you allow into your mind and as you fill your mind with them, you should realize that you are forming opinions about life that may just work against you!

Could you learn some new positive thoughts to change the old negative ones, before they change you anymore?

Remember that you are working to change a thinking and behavior pattern and to do this you must learn where your thinking patterns stem from, while remembering that deeds and conditions do not define a person, as a person with a condition is a person and not a condition.
You are always a person first and it is time to stop your mind from believing everything that you hear, or have heard, in regards to what or who you are and it is time to see the truth about all that you are becoming, as well as all that you can do to advance your new positive thinking life.
Your life is about to change through your decisions for change; so keep the thoughts positive, as you strive for positive change.

(Day 2) 1.1 #2 Erasing old programming.

To get the most out of new thinking and new life you need to start each new day with enough positive self talk to get a firm hold on your feelings and emotions, before they have a chance to get a hold of you. So you must learn to control your thoughts, as you retrain your brain to realize that living in an attitude controlled by feelings such as, "I feel", or "I can't" etc. is a decision that will only hinder your recovery.

It is time to change your thought processes and to choose your words and attitudes carefully, while continually looking forward and working towards a "yes I can" attitude. In preparing for these changes, you need to remember that you are deserving of a life free from addiction and negative behaviors and that self-recovery is real and is for you, if you will work for and believe in it, while believing in yourself.

As you start welcoming change, you will also learn to strengthen your mind through understanding where your thinking and thought patterns originated, but do not decide to wait until tomorrow to start your learning, as now is the time to stand up and make better decisions, while remembering that a bad decision is just a decision that you must take responsibility for and then take care of it in the best and most efficient manner possible; in other words, stand up to it, fix it, get over it and get rid of it. Forgive your mistakes and work to make your next decisions good ones, one decision at a time, until your life becomes flooded with good decisions.

You do harness the power of change and of a better life, through your decision making, but you have to be willing to participate fully and honestly and be able to understand why you think the way that you think and be willing to change when and where change is called for, as life change will come through retraining your brain, while eliminating the learned false knowledge, lies and myths that have been fed to your brain to lead you astray.

It is time to become fully conscious to the fact that your brain will believe, feel, or use, whatever you teach it, which includes positive affirmations, as well as the negative words, attitudes, actions, thoughts and persecutions that you speak, hear, see and continuously allow into your mind.

You must not waste any more time on dangerous negative thoughts and behaviors as you learn to erase the bad programming that has engulfed your confidence and imprisoned your true powers of recovery. It is time to empty the trash out of your mind and to become mindful of what you allow back in.

Remember that you make the final decisions about your day's events, which means that you are responsible for good and bad decisions alike and it is time to own up to and forgive the bad ones; so that you can work on changing and making your now life better by living in the wisdom of a new day and not in the pains and mistakes of yesterday.

So you must keep telling yourself about the things that you are changing and willing to change to better your life and then make a commitment to start changing these behaviors, by replacing them with positive thoughts. Be sure to keep telling yourself good things about yourself, as your brain will come to believe what you are feeding it, so feed it well and expect that it will treat you well. Stop telling yourself what has power over you and what you cannot control, because in all truth, only you can control your thoughts, good or bad and today you will be retraining your brain to this truth, while turning more of your negative thoughts into positive ones.

Remember that in order to change your thinking, as well as your behaviors; you will be doing many new thinking tasks to learn how and where your individual thinking patterns have come from, as well as how to change them. Remember that each task is important in understanding personal thinking processes, even when you do not understand how, or why, as sometimes unconventional change will come through unconventional thinking.

So think about the upcoming plans, thoughts, ideas and questions, while remembering that you are looking to learn where your beliefs originated, not to argue that you are right and another is wrong, but to be willing to learn and change, while being understanding of yourself, as well as others rights and beliefs, as we do not all have to believe the same things to become healed, from the bad things.

(Day 2b) **1.1 #2 study thought. Erasing old programming**

Why do you think that you believe the things that you believe? It is time to see where many of your decisions and beliefs are from and how they could be based on false knowledge, traditions, or hear say and you need to see how easy it may be to be led into beliefs or deceived, when you believe things out of convenience; e.g. "that's what I was told".

You must learn where your beliefs come from and why you believe what you believe, to be able to fully understand your thinking and your life.

Think about the following to see how your thinking could be manipulated and to learn how to change it? Be sure to remember that you are working on changing a thinking problem, not a drinking (drug) problem, as the drinking needs to end, but your thinking needs a new start.

A. In the political realm do you see yourself as a Democrat, Republican, or? Why? How did you come by your belief? The idea here is only to see why you believe what you believe and to be sure that it is outside of false common knowledge. Are your beliefs through facts or what you believe or have "knowledge" of? Did others help you to see what you are? Or is it just what you have always been? Regardless of the beliefs you probably do care more about politics than you realize and your voice does matter, as you are as much an important part of the community as any other, as it takes every part to make a whole and you are a part! What kind of a part is up to you?

Be assured that you are capable of finding and living the real truth, through courage, wisdom and questioning your beliefs, before just accepting that you are what you were told you are, as some of the things that you have been told could be false.

So again: Why do you believe what you believe? How did you come by these beliefs? And are you capable of and allowed to change your beliefs and still feel good about yourself?

B. What are your spiritual beliefs? Have you researched them? Who chose your basis for moral life? Were you brought up being told what you were? If your beliefs changed would you change? I found the courage to study and find my true self based on facts and though you may be just what you were told, make sure that you are deciding your beliefs based on fact, while remembering that life is not about arguing beliefs; it is about knowing why you believe what you believe and about being able to change, as you must be allowed to stand firmly on factual truths?

C. What about your beliefs about people, groups, cultures, life, alcohol, drugs, addiction, recovery etc.?
Are your beliefs from facts or do you ride on other's beliefs?
Were you taught what to believe, or to like/ dislike? Do you like/ not like certain people/things based on other's opinions? Is it just what you were taught to believe?
Are your beliefs based on your attitudes, or education? Do some people not fit the "ideals" that you judge them by? Why? Do you not fit the ideals that others were taught to falsely judge you by? Why? Which side of the tracks are you from? This shows how easy it is to get roped into false beliefs, when you are taught to believe what others think, as tracks are not made to separate people?

D. Are you a lost cause? An "alcoholic"? "Addict"? Burden to others? Who says so? Why? Do you believe this junk? Why? Just because another said so? Be assured that these are not just words; they are negative oppressive harmful labeling, as a person with an addiction is a person, not a dysfunctional or addicted person, or alchy or addict, but a person, maybe with a behavioral condition, but a person! No matter what anybody says, as others beliefs do not create truth and you owe it to yourself to know the real truth, not just what you have been told to be true.

So do you feel that you are dysfunctional? Do you know what dysfunctional means, not your assumption, but the truth?
If you find through new learning that you are okay, will you be willing to give yourself a chance to be functional?

(Day 3) 1.1 #3 Erasing old programming

You should be seeing that some of your "truths" may just be passed down beliefs, hearsay and traditions and it is time for these beliefs to be validated, changed, or disposed of, as you recognize how you could have fallen into others deceptions and how it can become an easy way to bypass things that should be dealt with, which could cause negative thoughts to become trapped in the unconscious mind, causing problems in the now and future life change processes.

This life change starts with brain retraining and eliminating self deception, false knowledge, lies and myths, through stopping the deception. Remember that your brain will believe, feel, or use whatever you teach it, which includes, not just the positive affirmations, but also all the negative words, attitudes, thoughts and lies that you speak, hear, see and allow into your mind; but you alone hold the power to stop this flood of false knowledge and to replace it with positive truths.

To get the most out your thinking you must start each day with enough positive self-talk to change the negative thoughts and feelings that you harbor. Start by choosing daily words and attitudes carefully, while continually working towards recovery. C.P.R. recovery will work for you, if you will work for it, by using your power to control emotions and reactions, while remembering that you have the right to change these feelings at any time, as well as to change your life, mind, friends, activities etc. as you have the full right to complete change anytime that you want to change.

Now if you are afraid of change than you will learn to change while being afraid, as feelings of fear are just feelings, so do not allow irrational fear to intimidate you against change. You will also find that you can change as often as you wish, without being considered indecisive; as indecisive says that I cannot make up my mind, whereas changing your mind says; I know what I want and it is different now than it once was. So keep building the courage, to keep making new decisions for your life, based solely on facts, responsibility and truths, as you are responsible for your life decisions and each decision will come to affect your life.

(Day 3b) **1.1 #3 study thought. Erasing old programming**

Consciously and honestly think about the following;

Whose truths are responsible for most of what you know?
Are you sure that the truths that you live by are not just another's false hearsay, or ideas, pressed into your beliefs?

What or who has the most influence over the things that you believe, say, feel and do? Why and how?

Why might it be important to know where your true and false beliefs come from? Are you willing to revalidate your beliefs?

Have changes in your thoughts and behaviors, caused changes in your life? Could changing them again, change you again?

What life changes might be needed to accomplish your goals? What can you do to implement these changes? How?

Who or what will decide your attitude for today? Will you give your power away by allowing others attitudes, words and actions to influence your feelings and life decisions?

Think about what you are willing to change in regards to your beliefs, be assured that learning about your belief system is "a good start" in understanding life needs, but a good start is just a start and it is time to follow through with "good change", by changing negative thoughts into positive actions.

To start getting the most out of your thinking; you will have to start each day with positive self-talk, as your mind and attitude will be affected by everything that you say.

Now is the time to start flooding your brain with good positive thinking and to lay to rest all the negative gossip, garbage and false truths, that others have talked you into believing and to stand away from those who are afraid of change, truth and responsibility, as you must learn to accept change, truth and responsibility into your C.P.R. recovery life.

(Day 4) 1.2 Knowledge vs. Wisdom

In working through life change it is going to be important to learn the difference between knowledge and wisdom, while discovering some new truths about your belief system.

Now is the time to start making new responsible life decisions while seeking to find the real truths that will guide your recovery. Be assured that you can be healed of any negative conditions, through your personal power of decision and that it will be through your hard work and these positive productive decisions that your life will be changed.

You have probably realized that there is a lot of knowledge in the world and though knowledge can be good, it does not equal wisdom or truth. So now you will learn how knowledge can also be false and potentially harmful, which is why you need to learn to be careful about buying into what others call knowledge and accept as truth.

You are also going to learn to stop fighting against yourself in the name of "knowledge", ego boosts, or fitting in with those whose beliefs may not come from factual truth.

This is where you will find how far into your own beliefs that you are willing to venture and if you are willing to admit that many of your beliefs may not be as true as you once thought. It is time to become open minded and to start accepting new factual truths about life and recovery; truths based on true knowledge and wisdom and not on false knowledge, myths or hearsay, as many people fall into this trap of living on invalidated knowledge and it is time to realize that just because a person makes a statement of knowledge, or has knowledge of something, that does not make the message in the statement true!

You can have knowledge of something without that something being validated or true, as no matter how many people stand by a belief, or common knowledge, if it is not proven factually true, than it could still be false.

Now if you desire true life change, than you must be willing to question all that you know as well as to realize that you may have taken in vast amounts of this false knowledge, including in regards to dependency and addiction myths and those that believe that you cannot quit this negative behavior.

Once you learn to question your beliefs and find your truths, then you can work on ending the oppression that you have been living under, which will come through discovering the true power of your personal decisions, personal responsibility and the wisdom to exchange false knowledge and common beliefs, for true knowledge and a belief in oneself, so as to be able to become free of the oppressions and myths of addiction, by eliminating common myths, lies and behaviors.

Remember that common knowledge only means that many people claim to know something, which does not equal truth, though this knowledge can harbor truths, or lies and includes thoughts about alcohol, drugs and addiction and how to live with, deal with or shun the blame for them.

So just because you have knowledge of something, or someone has told you something, does not mean that it is valid, useful or truthful knowledge. Remember that your brain only knows what you and society has fed it and now it is important to realize that while you were feeding your brain; that there were many negative, false and harmful thoughts, traditions, and lies coming into your life and it is possible that some of them were pressed into your unconscious mind, which in turn could cause one to believe that they were standing on truth, when in fact they may be standing in the dark, on false common knowledge, or hearsay.

I have heard that if you want to get out of the darkness, then you turn on the light; physically, or spiritually if you wish and though this may be knowledge, you may find that if you turn on a light, but do not open your eyes than you are still living in the dark; which means that hearing may bring knowledge, but seeking out the whole truth can bring wisdom. So when seeking to get out of the darkness of addiction, you must make a plan and you must work it, decision by decision, in all truth, while remembering each detail, including remembering to open your eyes and your mind, as well as the eyes to your mind, as the time to seek out the full truth and to start taking full responsibility is now.

Always live by the wisdom of truth, because a truth that hurts will always be better and more productive than a lie that falsely comforts.

(Day 4b) **1.2 #1 study thought. Knowledge vs. Wisdom**

In thinking about the following, be factual and logical, not excuse making, or argumentative, as you are working to learn about your own beliefs; not to impose them onto others.

Have you ever claimed a personal belief as truth, to later find that you were wrong? How did you handle it? If this happened now, would you, learn the truth and make amends? How? Or would you just say "oh well no one's perfect"?

Have you ever shared (false) knowledge that insinuates that drinking is okay? Why? e.g. To relax, fit in, avoid arguments?

Have you made arguments for using alcohol, drugs, pills, or other negative life choices? Why?

What excuses do you use to argue your "right" to do as you wish? Are they logical or rational excuses? Do you believe them? Do you expect others to believe your excuses? Why?

How will you admit to, apologize for and take responsibility for your mistakes, false thoughts, excuses and bad decisions?

Do you think or say that one drink can never hurt? Or that it can help you relax? Do you believe these excuses? Why?

Are there other things that can help you relax? Could changes in your attitude, thoughts and thinking help you? How?

Can you see why people may not invest in you, if you will not invest in yourself? What can you do to show that you are serious about life changes? When will you start?

It may help in thinking about what you can do, by thinking about what you may need. Following are some examples:

A. Do you feel a need for someone to understand your fears and all the bad that has been happening in your life?

You may find that you are the one that you need to understand your thoughts, fears and needs to become capable of fully understanding yourself, before expecting others to. So what changes can you make to show yourself and others that you are willing to learn how to help yourself?

B. Do you need to know how to get back to "normal life" after doing so much wrong? It is time to learn how to follow a plan of action to increase your true wisdom and to understand life better, as life is a plan and though it does not have to be followed perfectly, it needs to be followed honestly.
Are you willing to create a life plan that works with you and for you? What can you do to start building your plan?

C. Do you need to be understood for who you are and not by what you are labeled, due to past deeds of desperation? Remember when separating the person from the deed that you are also a person and though you need to forgive others, you must forgive yourself first and realize that others who care about you may just be waiting for you to show that you can care about yourself before they become involved and invest their efforts and care into your life.

D. Do you need people to understand that it is not your fault that your life turned the direction that it did; this will not happen without accepting responsibility for your decisions and finding the courage to turn your behaviors around?
You can start by admitting that these are learned behaviors and as such, can and will be unlearned by you and your efforts?

You are going to find that the only person who truly understands you and your fears is the person that you need to understand you the most, which is you!

You are the person that matters the most in your recovery and your life and you must realize that nobody can love and help you like you can; so stop being judgmental and give yourself a chance at the life that you deserve, because you are the one person that you cannot live without and nobody can give you, what you have to offer yourself.

(Day 5) 1.2 #2 Knowledge vs. Wisdom

I learned the hard way about factual truth, as I stood on false knowledge and beliefs and searched for any thoughts or people that were okay with me being "not okay", until one day I realized how wrong I had been by falling into the mindset of woe, with tales of woe, days of woe, nights of woe, woe is me, until I said woe; enough is enough and I realized that I had to find a way to get better. I realized that if it was okay to accept being not okay, than it must be okay, to be okay and it was time to leave the woe of addiction thinking behind and to find a path of recovery to rejoin with those who could teach me how to fit in and be okay as a responsible sober person.

I needed to find the wisdom to change my learned compulsive drinking behaviors and to find the power to live like the sober minded people had learned to and this is exactly what you will have to do. You will also need to learn to respect yourself, flaws and all and then you will be looking onward and forward and when it comes time, others respect for you will fall into place, or not, but either way, others respecting you is not your first goal, learning to respect yourself through your life decisions is.

Remember that you can forgive and respect a person without condoning the deeds, which includes yourself, as faults and blame have nothing to do with recovery, moving forward into a positive productive life of responsible decision making does. So forgive yourself and forgive your past deeds, because they are gone and you need to start looking towards making your next decisions ones that will help lift you up and out of the behavioral condition of addiction, because it is you that has to decide to leave the oppression, excuses and lies behind and to stand up and say; I am a person and flaws and all, I will achieve full recovery and become the best person that I can be for myself, by my standards; not for others, or their standards for me.

Remember that you are not looking for those that can help you to live and function with addiction, you are looking to live free from addiction and to become functional, as a viable person, not a functional addict. This means that you need to be cautious of those who use a false "common knowledge" for labeling, grouping or tearing persons down through their addiction myths, instead of lifting them up through recovery truths, as though many of these labelers may be sober, that does not mean that they have any better answers about their own lives, much less how to show what you need to be successful in yours.

So it is time to learn to not base your life on others judgments about you, or your life. Others may have the right to their beliefs, but you surely have the right to the truth and this is about you and your walk with the truth and you are going to find that knowing what others think, or can do for you, may not do you any good, because no matter how much you respect another or how much knowledge and love they offer you, this knowledge may not help, if it is based on tradition, myths or hearsay.

It is time that you understand the difference between true knowledge, common knowledge, tradition and wisdom and to understand that knowledge, or tradition, does not equal truth or wisdom and often is no more valid, than old wives tales, gossip or hearsay and can be more harmful than well thought out lies. So be ever mindful in reading through your plans, while remembering that the more truths and the more positives that you learn and teach your brain, the stronger and more positive your inner life will become.

You need to learn to question knowledge if you plan on seeking wisdom, because the wise person proves that which is good and works to change that which is wrong, because again, knowledge in itself is not always truth and even when it is, it may not be useful and can be harmful.

So do not live by the truths that you believe, live by truths that are factual and proven and not just what you have been told by someone that you trust. Remember that handed down truths, seem to pick up distortions as they move down the line and you do not have any more room to be taking any more chances with your life, so take the time to prove the truths that you intend on living by, because it is your life and it is that important.

(Day 5b) **1.2 #2 study thought. Knowledge vs. Wisdom**

Do you believe all that you claim to be true, is really truth? If not, why would you live by, repeat, or claim it to be true?

Can you accept that your knowledge may not be all that you believe it to be? Is it okay for you to have been wrong? Why? How do you act/ react when you are wrong? Why?

Are you open to researching the "truths" that you have been taught which may not be factual, even though you have lived as they are, or may wish them to be?
How will you check the validity of the truths that you live by?

Can you think of some things that you believe, or assume to be true, even though you have no proof that they are factual?

Think about the following, but do not take them out of context, as you are just being asked why you believe what you believe?
Do you believe that because you were taught and believed something that it must be truth? Could you have been taught someone else's false belief?

Do you believe everything that your parents told you? Why? Could they be capable of false knowledge? Why or why not?

Do you believe if you learned it in church that it's true? Could they teach their truth instead of Gods? I believe every word of the Bible, as God intended, just not everybody else's rendition.

Do you believe all that is taught about substance abuse to be true, or could there be false knowledge about addiction?

Do you believe that many teach a truth that fits the needs of an ideal society, even though we are not an ideal society?

Do you believe everything that friends tell you? Could it be hearsay, or things that they want to or want you to believe because it is what they were told and believe?

Many people accept others truths on faith, but now your life is on the line and it is time to start proving what you are willing to accept and to show that you are okay admitting that you have been and may be wrong in some of your beliefs.

Could the following statement be true, about you?

A lot of what I know I was told and there may be many things that I claim to be true, that I could be wrong about. I start some conversations with, so and so said, and I like to put my two cents in, but now I see that some of my "truths" may not be worth two cents and though this may hurt my ego, I would rather know and relay truth and have factual knowledge, than to lie. Many times what we believe we have "knowledge about", we simply have "knowledge of" from being told something, but being told something does not equal truth and it is time to understand the difference between what we have heard or want to be true and what is truth.

How might you start eliminating traditional addiction thinking knowledge from your life? What do you know or believe about self affirmations? e.g. "I can quit drinking" "I will quit drinking" "It is my decision" "I am a good person" and I will accept responsibility for my actions, but I will not accept being judged or labeled by another and even though I can understand others ignorance and will not argue, I also will not accept being told that I cannot do, what I need to do, to better my life, through my powers and my decisions.

Pay attention to the new thoughts and the old traditions that you hear from yourself and others, do not be judgmental and do not try being a great ball of wisdom; just pay attention, think mindfully and ask lots of questions of yourself and others; do not argue and do not force your knowledge onto others, as it is okay for them to believe differently, just not for them to impose their invalidated unproven beliefs onto you and remember that you are not going to argue your way sober; so put your ego to rest and operate on truths, good thoughts and true wisdom.

(Day 6) **1.2 #3 Knowledge vs. Wisdom**

By questioning your knowledge you will find the power to bring change into your life, through your good decisions, which often work by default, which means that you do not have to feel them working, for them to be working. You do need to prepare for new decisions, as many of the feelings, which precipitate the need for these decisions, will try to tear you down before you have a chance to change. So become prepared and when negative feelings come, you will be able to keep making good positive decisions, until the positive attitude and feeling reappears, through your own good thoughts.

As you are building your knowledge base and learning about your true self; you are going to find some who oppose your quest towards a new life, just remember that this is about you changing your life and that others are not partnering with you or looking to change with you and may not even care to see you change. So stop basing your life on what others tell you that you can or cannot do, even if you have to do it on your own.

This is your life and you may have to start out on your own, but remember that feeling alone is, is just another feeling and is still better than being in the wrong place, with the wrong people. Teach yourself to use your alone time wisely, by viewing it as thinking time, which can be used to tell yourself positive self affirmations; and then even being alone, will be productive and good, by your decision.

It is by your decisions, knowledge and ability that you will achieve recovery, as you realize that you are just a person who got caught up in a behavioral condition, but who will not give in to common knowledge about alcohol, addiction, recovery, or life, because many times common knowledge is no more than the hearsay of a group that only knows what they have been told and what they have been told is not what you will be basing your life change and recovery on.

Remember that this is for your recovery, so be mindful while building your foundation on factual truth and good decisions, as your next decision is yours to make and you need to become responsible and make it to live free of the bondages of bad decision making.

(Day 6b) **study thought 1.2 #3. Knowledge vs. Wisdom**

It is time to stop thinking about yesterday's faults, or tomorrow's possibilities and concentrating on today's next decision, as life starts now and stays in the now, with every decision that you make and it is harmful to use yesterday and tomorrow to excuse what needs done today. If your kids were hungry, would you figure they were "bad" yesterday, so they can eat tomorrow, or would this be illogical in relation to what is important, like today and right now? Would you tell your boss you worked yesterday and will tomorrow, but today is a hectic so we'll see? How about life sustaining medicine you did the yesterday and tomorrow thing, so why bother today?
What about quitting drinking? Yesterday was bad, today is no good, maybe start fresh tomorrow? When does tomorrow get here? When you die? Can you see why you must make today's decisions for today and must do it right now, because tomorrow is a lie and tomorrow never gets here?

Along with the illogical thinking of tomorrow, think about the following false common knowledge, which may help you to see why you need to become more mindful in your thinking?

A. Substance abuse programs must work, because the courts send people to them? What can you see wrong with this kind of thinking? What decides truth for you?

B. Are forced programs based on recovery, responsibility, or punishment? Can the program change you, or does it just give you a chance to change yourself? As it is still you that makes the decision, learns and pays or benefits from your choices?

C. Helping programs are all over so they must work, right?
Plentiful does not mean works? Programs do not work, they are meant to teach, but you must be willing to learn and work.
 Get the facts about recovery programs, not arguments, as good programs do not need arguments, they need foundation; such as C.P.R., whose foundation is truth, responsibility and self recovery. I know the truths and I will stand by them, even when it goes against common beliefs.

(Day 7) **1.3 I am a person**

Today you will learn more about your powers and how to keep them working for you, as you are going to need them for your full recovery to be effective. You will need to start using these powers to help eliminate the oppressive negative thoughts that you have been feeding your mind, as well as working to eliminate all the falsehoods and myths that you have heard about yourself and addiction.

It is time to start living on factual truths, as you work to become the person that you are capable of becoming, while discovering new truths about your life. So you must be willing to make the decision to change your life, through changing your thinking, as you learn that you are a person that is capable of life change; through the decision to be a better person, by living a better life, starting with your next decision.

You are going to find that you are a whole person with a lot of potential power and that you can be healed, once you learn how to use this power of change, through your good decision making ability. It is time to use this power to ensure that you will come through today, a different and better person than you were yesterday, as this is the best day of your life, if you choose to see it as such, as it is a choice.

You must believe that you are capable of change in all your thinking, while fully expecting this change to positively affect your full recovery, because if you were not expecting life to be better, than why would you invest yourself.

You have already made an investment, of yourself, into a negative lifestyle and if you want to admit it or not, your investment has changed you and your life and now it is going to take another investment of your thinking and decision making skills to counteract these negative learned behaviors.

You can be assured that with your new investment that you will be changed again, with the difference being that this time you will be using your powers to positively affect your life and to achieve full recovery, as now is the time to start becoming the person that you are capable of becoming, free of the oppression of what others say that you are.

Be assured that most everyone has behaviors that need changed and you are no different, except that now you are willing to stand up, admit to and learn how to change your behavioral tendencies, as you now have the capability of change and will be starting by stopping; starting by stopping the use of oppressive language and labels in your thinking, as you now know that what you tell your brain matters and you do not want to fill your mind with anything that takes away from the worthwhile individual that you truly are.

You are a worthwhile person, with a behavioral condition, which will be changed, nothing more nothing less. Yes you may have spent years living a negative lifestyle, but that is past and does not make you anything other than a person, that is worth saving and teaching how to enjoy the fruits of a responsible lifestyle.

So join with me in admitting to being a worthwhile person; as even though I drank obsessively and compulsively for many years, I am a person; now I too allowed myself to be treated as an outcast for some time before I found my C.P.R. recovery and found that I was and am a person with a new beginning, each and every day and a past that is where it belongs; changed, forgiven and gone, melted away in the desert to never be seen again.

Stop accepting negative opinions about your tendencies right now, as you owe it to yourself to not accept negative treatment and even though others have the right to their opinions, that does not mean that you have to accept them, because others false beliefs do not dictate who you are and are not what you are basing your life on.

You must also realize that giving in to others false knowledge about your life does not diminish your responsibility, so do not give in to thinking that gives some false sense of reprieve for your decisions and actions, because if you want true change than you need to start calling yourself what the truth says that you are, which is a person who has made some mistakes and who now has some new decisions to make about taking responsibility and moving beyond the oppressive side of addiction and who is fully capable of doing what it takes to get to where you need to be.

(Day 7b) **1.3 #1 study thought. I am a person**

Remember that you are not working to become a sober, or any other kind of alcoholic, but to become a person who learns to use their power to change the negative thoughts and behaviors that have been hindering life. These thinking changes may be difficult, as often it is hard to think about, or to do, what is right, but these changes are a must, as you work towards a full life through full recovery.

Think about the following and add your thoughts, while remembering that you are responsible for your adult decisions.

A. How many <u>excuses</u> can you think of to use alcohol and drugs? e.g. I am an alchy, I have a hard life, I'm depressed, someone died, everyone does it, it was free, I was mad, sad, happy, It feels good, I work hard, lost a job, got a job, I get scared, it was a party, it felt like the thing to do, it can't hurt, I needed to get away, I deserve it, that's how we celebrate, mourn, relax etc.

B. Now, how many <u>good</u> <u>reasons</u> can you think of to use these substances? I could not find any? But say what comes to mind, just be honest, as out of the thousands of reasons that you can find to drink, how many are truly good and how many are lies? Be careful to not turn bad excuses into reasons by convincing your mind to believe that it is an okay reason, when in reality you drink because of a decision, regardless of the reasons or excuses, that you have convinced yourself of.

C. Try thinking about reasons and excuses that you can think of to not drink, be as liberal as when making excuses to drink. e.g. Maybe I will not drink today because? I have not found a bad, or sad enough excuse to harm myself, I was not fired, because I choose not to, I am stronger than temptation, because my family is worth more than a bottle, keep thinking because there are no irrelevant reasons, as can be seen when you change them around for excuses to drink, even though "that's different" and is the kind of thinking that you need to change.

D. Do you believe that you cannot quit drinking on your own? Why? Think about the question again, because it does not say that you cannot quit, it says that you cannot quit "on your own", which still insinuates that you can quit, with help. Try C.P.R. and instead of believing that you cannot quit, start making the decisions to believe that you can quit, either on your own, or with help and just because you can.

Start stopping right now, by telling your brain and unconscious what you can and will do, "I will quit for me", "I do not expect it to be easy, but I can still do it"; and then do it.

E. Do you need to be around people who understand your addiction? Why? I would think that being around people who can model proper behaviors, good living and who may be able to offer positive helpful resources may be a good idea, what do you think? If you wanted to quit sinning would you hang out with sinners telling you about all their wicked adventures?

You could do better by being around those who do not care to understand addiction thinking, as you do not plan to keep this bad thinking, that you also do not understand and if you intend on thinking and living better, wouldn't it seem sensible to be around people who could show you how to do that?

It is time to realize that you are an adult and you are going to have to give up past ways, for new beginnings, as you are the most important person in your life and you have to do what is best for you, so it is time to see that hanging around people stuck in addiction, only reinforces addiction, at a time when you should be concentrating on reinforcing recovery.

So start looking within and trusting yourself for the decisions and actions needed for your recovery and stop hanging around where excuses and labels flow freely, when you could be using your wisdom and powers to keep yourself out of potentially negative situations, while also realizing that true friends will understand and will not do anything to hinder your decision to break this negative part of your old lifestyle.

(Day 8) **1.3 #2 I am a person**

You must learn to take responsibility and admit that you are a person in need of thinking and lifestyle changes. It may be hard, but again you can start by acknowledging yourself as a worthwhile individual who has found themselves caught up in a whirlwind of bad decision making and lies, but who is willing to work towards change for a better today. It is time to own your decisions and to make amends for the way you have allowed your thoughts and other's oppressive ideals to control you, as you must acknowledge that drinking is a decision that you have made and call it what it is, a bad decision.

It is time for the mature, truthful you, to admit that this pathway to destructive thinking has been caused by your decisions. Saying that it is not you that has caused your problems is the lie, that you try to force your mind to believe, but the truth is that your choices and actions caused and are causing your problems and now it is time to take responsibility by making the decision to not drink that next drink.

This is worth repeating, because if you are ready to get sober then you have to be ready to hear the truth, as even though you may have wasted part of your life, with alcohol or other drugs, your life is not ruined, it may be in disarray but most damages can be repaired with time and what cannot be is just a fact of life, so move on to the things that can be changed.

Your next good decisions are waiting to be made and it is up to you on how long you will wallow in self pity, allowing it to control your decisions, thoughts, and life, before you reclaim control through your good rational decisions.

It is time to view your life honestly, so stop making excuses and trying to refocus the blame for your abuse, because accept it or not, it was and is your decision, no matter what the reasoning. You had to decide to say yes or no and now it is time to decide that this feeling of being defeated and helpless has got to go and the only way to get rid of it, is by realizing that the next decision is yours and you need to become responsible and make it to live free of the bondages of bad decisions and then you will know that the truly responsible decision is the decision to not drink.

The truth is that anyone can be healed of negative addiction thinking once they become ready to learn to admit the truth about why they do what they do and to stop laying blame on the objects of the addiction. Be assured the bottle did not drink you, it could not force you, it did not tip you, attack you, talk to you, or any of the other bad negative thoughts that you unwittingly use without realizing what you are teaching your brain to believe.

Remember, you cannot truly be healed, or respected, if you will not take responsibility for your life and become ready to accept the positive change that you must work for. In seeking recovery, you will learn dependence on your own good decision making skills, abilities and responsibilities, as you remember that you are seeking a path away from dependence and that the only thing that you can allow your recovery to be somewhat dependent on is your good decisions.

It is time to break free of oppressive name calling and admit that you are a person, maybe that no one wants to understand at the moment, but still a person. You may be a person who is a compulsive drinker, but you are a person and once you make the decision to not drink, you will be a person, who has decided to stay sober and who at sometime in their life had exercised bad judgment by their own decision, but who was still a person, who now by the power of good decisions chooses not to drink.

Compulsiveness is a behavioral condition, which means that if you change your behavior, such as drinking, then you change the condition and once the condition and behavior are changed, then the person and the life is changed. The compulsive drinker has this power to change the behavior, which changes the condition and results in life change through better decision making and social networking.

Remember that even life changing decisions are just decisions and it is time to start making them to become responsible, as well as to break free of the bondages of those who would have you believe that you are incapable of controlling your life. So quit feeding on negatives, with those who choose to live under the oppression of others and get ready to start recognizing and using your true powers for your true C.P.R. and full recovery.

(Day 8b) **1.3 #2 study thought. I am a person**

Be very mindful when thinking about life questions and remember that what is important is to realize where your beliefs originated from and why you believe what you believe.

What do you believe an "alcoholic" or "addict" to be? Why? Are you sure that what you have been told is true? According to whom? Does that make it true? Why or why not? Is the person the "ic" part? What does "ic" stand for?
Are you a "person" who drank alcohol, or are you a club member for alcohol that names its members after that which you want to get away from, alcohol-"?ics" Why doesn't everyone believe the same thing? Who is right? Why?

Some call drinking a disease, in part from the criteria of: craving, dependency, tolerance, preoccupation withdrawal. Have you ever felt these towards anything else? Does that make them diseases? Are drinking or drugging diseases? Why? If you quit, is the disease gone? Or will you always be diseased or have you actually never been? Is it a d_sease, or a d_cision

Do you know the differences in a problem, condition, choice, disease, decision, tradition or fact of life? I will tell you that, choices are yours, tradition is from others and a fact of life is something that you cannot change.

Drinking and living with addiction is not a fact of life, as you are not stuck in it and it is not a problem that needs fixed; it is a condition that needs changed through your decision to change.

Think about the following and if you would define them as disease, problem, condition, choice, tradition, or fact of life.

A. I cannot quit drinking on my own. Why? Because you were told you can't, so you choose to believe that you can't? If you tell your brain that you cannot quit, that is not truth, that is self fulfilling prophecy and you may not quit because of it.
Think how saying I cannot, could be a problem, a condition, a choice, or a fact of life (falsely through one's power).

B. I am an alcoholic and that is just a fact of life. Remember that saying that something is a fact does not make it a fact! It may be fact that there will always be people with negative behavioral tendencies, but that does not make the tendency a fact of life.

C. I have caused many problems with past drinking. This is not a problem, as it is past and you cannot do anything about it, which means, it is a fact of life that you will have to come to terms with and forgive. You can do better and make amends, for the past, in the now, but do not let your past ruin your now.

D. I have been a bad person! So stop being a bad person, start with your next decision. You cannot change your past decisions, but you can change your next ones and you can live better today, by getting out of yesterday and tomorrow. Time can change many things but you must change your behaviors, which will come through your good thoughts and decisions.

You must stand up, take responsibility, shoulder the blame and do your part in breaking this temporary addiction cycle that you are moving out of and be assured that addiction is temporary, as you have not always been this way and do not intend on staying this way, so even if you have been this way "forever", it is still temporary and time to learn how to quit it.

Stop living by feelings, false beliefs, hearsay, tradition and all that works against the truth, as you have caused your problems and it will be your decisions that fixes them, by recognizing them for what they are, knowing how they came about and changing your thoughts, feelings and decisions, so as to change your life back into a life of truth and recovery, in the now.

Now is the time for you to find your life truths and to remember that truth is truth and that alcohol cannot be blamed for your actions, no matter what others tell you, as it is time to stop looking for what you want to hear and start telling yourself what you need to hear, which is the truth, the whole truth and nothing but the truth! You must start living by the truth.

(Day 9) **1.3 #3 I am still a person**

With this decision to be a better person and to live a better life, you will start modeling confident behaviors and good direction, regardless of outer circumstances. The goal here is not just abstinence; it is about how to live a better life through taking responsibility for your decisions. It is about believing in you and letting go of and forgiving yesterday, so that a fresh new start is possible. It is about understanding that life may not get easier, but it can be better. It is about you starting your comeback by seeking answers and by looking to have a better understanding of life and with C.P.R. you have found a true new chance, based on your decisions and powers and your life.

Do not worry about other chances that you feel you have used up, as they are past and were not true chances. Remember that your success is going to be because of you and your decisive power to do and be better, while learning to take life, one decision at a time. This is a chance for a better life and a plan to get you thinking constructively and to learn to live free of the bondages of addiction, as you learn to rely on your true senses.

You must decide right now to do what it takes to no longer allow drugs to invade your life and to quit living to be acceptable to others. It is time to realize that you are probably a better person than you give yourself credit for, so learn to accept yourself, flaws and all, as having others need you, like you, or care about you is nice, but it is not a necessity; accepting yourself is. So do not give up your life goals, dreams or quest, just because someone else does not seem to care; not everybody is going to care about you, that is life, but it is your life and what is important is that you learn to care about yourself, because liking, loving, needing and caring about yourself, is a necessity for maximizing your full life potential.

For new beginnings you have to find the courage to do what is best, while forgiving the past. There are many decisions to make and being hurt in, or having a tragic past is no reason to live in despair. Past hurts can only hold you down if you allow them to, because like addiction, mental pain gets its power from you allowing it to distress your life, which means that if you stop feeding it the negative thoughts that it thrives on, it will dissipate. The past cannot drag you down; you are the one that drags it around and lets it choke the life out of you, until you learn to let go and to live beyond the harmful influences, feelings and excuses that it has bound to your life.

So be sure, as you move out of the tragic mindset of hurt, pain, addiction and I can't, that you are preparing your whole self to stand strong against any outside forces that may come against your new thinking, as it is time for you to bear down against these negative attitudes and stand firm in your C.P.R. recovery, because only you can hold onto and build on your foundation of recovery.

Most of C.P.R. will be on changing behavioral conditions, decision making processes, thoughts, feelings and attitudes relating to your inner being, which is where the bulk of your positive changes are going to manifest, but there is another part of you that we are going to take a few minutes to discuss and that is the physical you, as it is time to start paying attention to every aspect of your life, which includes the physical, biological, psychological and social you.

This condition has changed and or affected more than just your inner life. It has caused changes in social habits, eating, health care, anxiety and stress levels and though we will not address all the issues, we will discuss a couple, because as you seek change, you need to make sure that you think about all the parts of your life and work on and accept change in every part.

As you are seeking to become a whole person you will be bringing the whole bio-psychosocial you into the equation, because every part of you and your life, affects every part of you and your life. Your diet affects your mental health, your health care habits affect your physical and social life, your breathing affects your stress and anxiety etc. The point is that if you want change in your life than you need to be ready for change and ready to do and hear things differently, which must include your entire world.

Remember that self-recovery is not about changing all at once, nor is it about the past, future, or living a year, week or day at a time and is not about what others believe, it is about learning to live one good decision at a time and realizing that every next decision that you make is the most important decision that you have to make.

(Day 9b) **1.3 #3 study thought. I am a person**

You will become better each day, as you offer the patience to yourself to do so; while realizing that setbacks will come, but as long as you stay focused and moving forward than setbacks can and will be dealt with and disposed of effectively.

One thing that can assist in your life focus and good mental and physical health is checking with your doctor about proper healthy breathing techniques, which can greatly assist in lessening the feelings of anxiety and stress, by helping you to learn how to lower stress levels and remain calm, which is a key factor when facing changes in one's learned way of life.

Conscious breathing can be used with positive visualizations, in which you use calming thoughts and visions, or calming words, with deep breathing to face stressful situations. The breathing is done from the stomach and is referred to as slow diaphragmatic (from the stomach, <u>not the chest</u>)breathing and is done in through the nose and out through the mouth, while counting to four, which can slow heart rate, regulate oxygen and reduce feelings of anxiety, stress and anger. Seek a doctor's advice, especially if you have breathing, heart or asthma issues and then start paying close attention to your breathing throughout the day, while using your positive self talk. Remember with this breathing the stomach rises, not the chest as chest breathing can cause feelings that mimic anxiety.

Keep your mind on your goals, as you move beyond your feelings, and work to change your life into a positive, forward moving, sober network of positive interdependencies, which means that you must become committed to healthy thinking and living by your power of good decision making, so that when life gets tough, you get tougher and calmer, as you now counteract negative behavior through self talk and breathing.

It is also time to realize that happiness is a personal decision and that you do not have to be happy with outer experiences to experience inner peace, because it is your decision how you choose to feel today and with a good attitude and good decisions, you can become happier with yourself, your day and your life by your decision to do so.

Choose wisely what you decide to think, feel and say today, as what you thought yesterday, or last week has no bearing on your now life and what you once believed does not make you what you are today. Remember, beliefs do not create truths, even though you can make yourself feel bad with false ones.

With C.P.R. you will take control of your thoughts and decisions and fill your time with new positive talk, such as how you can comeback better than you have ever been and could feel and do better just because it is in your power to; so you must remain an active part of your recovery and concentrate on controlling your emotions, feelings and decisions in the now, as this is not about yesterday, or who or what you used to be, or was told you were, it is about who and what you are becoming and in part, about what you are willing to do to accomplish your life goals.

Once you find the courage to do what is best for you, than you are going to have to take action to keep the temptations associated with these behaviors at bay, remember that when life is tough, it is not only tough on you, but you are the one who has to change how it affects you, through your positive traits of self discipline, obedience, self talk and good decisions.

Start everyday with positive productive self-talk, regardless of the circumstances and regardless of how you think you feel, as you can take control of life and make it good; in and through your own thought processes, decisions and feelings, as your mind only knows and acts on what you teach it, so start teaching it that you are going to make life what you need it to be for you.

Teach your mind that life is good and you can learn to see life as good; then unbury all the good thoughts about you, which have been buried for too long, as it is by your decisions, knowledge, ability and power that you will achieve full powerful productive self recovery and new beginnings.

(Day 10) **1.4 Sober thinking and thinking sober**

To understand sober thinking skills you need to be open to asking yourself some sobering questions, while being prepared to discover some sobering truths.

Now is the time to start making responsible decisions, forgiving the past and learning to see things differently than you may be used to, as you are going to work hard to get sober minded and to abstain from compulsion. There will be times that you may feel alone, or afraid, but you will learn to live beyond these and other harmful feelings, while moving your thoughts away from self doubt. So keep moving and looking forward, through doubt and fear, and victory will be yours.

The goal here is to move beyond the negative feelings associated with addiction thinking and to change your life into a forward moving sober network of good decision making, regardless of the feelings, which means that you must become committed to sober thinking, while keeping thinking sober.

It is time to prove yourself smarter than what you believe and to stop being led down the wrong paths, as you know behavioral instigators, like alcohol or drugs, have the ability to diminish self control and to cause you to alter your path in life, but remember that it is you that holds the power and makes the decision to alter or change the path that you are on.

Alcohol and other drugs can confuse sober thinking skills and sway lives, but they carry no physical power, no matter what others false beliefs tell you, as belief does not create truth and the truth is that alcohol does not exert control, people exert control and when things are bad and there is no one to blame, the drinking thinking mind tries to shift the blame, but this does not diminish your responsibility.

Individuals can fall into negative self defeating behaviors through many different feelings and excuses. Many may feel that they deserve a break, or a need to cover up life's ills and errs, but no matter what the excuse, it usually involves the "poor me" "I feel" "life's hard on me", feeling self, which thrives on feelings and fear of inadequacy and it is time to get over this poor me feeling and negative addiction thinking self and leave your ego based pity party behind.

If you have decided to entertain a feeling that you have done terrible things and do not deserve to feel better, then now is the time to put these feelings to rest, as you must get over all negative behavioral thinking. Now you may have done terrible things, but that is then and you live in the now and you deserve and have every chance to do better in the now.

Maybe you feel that you have done good things and deserve a reward, but make the decision to move beyond this thinking and realize that your reward is sober thinking and being able to choose to be sober minded and to be in control of your powers, your life, your thinking and your decisions.

Be assured that most people have had good and bad thoughts about themselves or others, but you no longer live by these feelings, so do not let them take up room in your mind, as deserving or not has nothing to do with making the right decision for a better life. "I feel that I deserve" is no excuse to abuse your mind and body. You may deserve many things, but you do not reward yourself by poisoning your mind and body.

It is beyond logic to consider alcohol a reward, or a gift, or to feel like you would deserve anything so damaging, especially at the expense of your life, your sanity, your family and others who have to deal with your behaviors, so be very careful with the excuse that you deserve anything, as what you deserve and need is logical sober thinking and your next decisions working to guide your new day.

This sober thinking that you are moving towards is a mature thought out decision making process, which will be used to eliminate the irresponsible imaginary thoughts, feelings and behaviors that are standing in the way of your full recovery. As you move beyond this drinking thinking, you will learn to use your powers of good decision making to become grounded in the good sober thinking that will guide you through recovery.

This new thinking will move you beyond the negatively charged feelings that addiction thinking brings and as you move beyond these and change your life into a positive, forward moving, sober network of good decisions, you will become committed to sober thinking and making responsible decisions for your life, as you learn to live beyond the drinking thinking feelings of addiction.

(Day 10b) 1.4#1 study thought. Sober thinking thinking sober

Thinking sober has to do with being sober, which does not make you a logical rational thinker, yet it is a prerequisite for the "sober thinking" needed to learn to live beyond ones feelings. So thinking sober does not guarantee good thinking, but sober thinking does and is always rational.
So start your new day sober, while thinking sober and live the day with rational, logical, good, sober thinking.

You will change your thinking, by changing what you feed your mind, as you learn to live by what is real and not by what you feel. "I feel like" is a relative emotional response and it is time to stop allowing these thoughts to guide your life.
Learn to live beyond the feeling and see what sober thinking says. "But I don't feel like it! You do not have to feel like it, to just do it" "but I feel that__?" Does feeling it, make it true?

How does it make you feel to be told that your feelings are wrong? Could they be wrong? Think about it, admit it and move on, as you no longer live by feelings, which have nothing to do with logic, truth or sober thinking. Think logically, not by illogical feelings; move beyond "I feel" and into what's real and when the feeling tries to change you, look and live beyond it.

Listen to the things that you say and think about how they could be interpreted by your mind and before you think that it is just "small talk", remember that what your mouth considers small talk, your mind may see as truth, or lies. The unconscious is complicated and with the changes that you are facing, your mind needs all the help that you can offer, including being conscious of what you are saying and filling it with.

Think about what you honestly feel and what you tell your mind, such as, "I feel like the world is against me", as it is not, "If I do not drink I will go crazy", as you will not, "others are better than me", as they are not, "I am buried in too deep", as you are not. You take it from here, what are some of the things that you say you feel like; or that feels right or wrong for you?

It is time to realize that feelings have nothing to do with rational sober thinking, as the "I feel" parts can add illogical or negative thinking to your thought process. e.g. "I feel like if I do not drink I will go crazy". Now take away the "feeling part" and you have "if I do not drink I will go crazy" which is false, but your brain only knows what you have told it and if it is said enough times it will believe it to be true.

So now you must change the lies that you have instilled into your unconscious mind, into logical sober truths, such as changing, "I feel like if I do not drink I will go crazy" into, "if I do not drink I will get sober, of which I do need to rethink how to think soberly and to careful with what I say to my brain".

Repeating and believing positive thoughts may not bring immediate change, but it will start changing your thinking and by adding positive thoughts, you add inspiration, just as negative thoughts add anxiety and stress and could make productive thinking difficult.
So changing your talk, will change your life.
Change the talk and you change the thought and once you change the thought, you can change the feeling and once you change the feeling, then you can change the behavior. So take the thoughts away from the feelings and feelings away from the thoughts and then you can change the behavior, through the power of self talk and your decision to do better.

Start eliminating negative thoughts and feelings by replacing them with positives, just because you can. Think about this exchange like buying something; if it is bad when you receive it, then it is logical to exchange it for better.
So now do the same with those bad things in your mind, e.g. all the negative thoughts and ideas that you receive daily and have received over the years; if they are bad, do not keep them or bury them, exchange them for a good thought and do not waste time trying to convince yourself how hard it is to forgive some things, as that is just more of the bad thinking that needs exchanged for the truth, of how easy it is to forgive, because forgiveness is a decision in your mind, made by you, so if it feels hard, do it anyways by the power of your decision.

(Day 11) 1.4#2 Sober thinking/ thinking sober

Think about some of the decisions that you make every day and about what you base your decisions on. Do you just get through the day, doing what you do to please the needful ego based you, or do you think soberly about your true beliefs and what would be best for you, or do you actually take the time to think rationally and mindfully and soberly, while realizing that every word, thought and decision that comes through you, can affect what is best for you.

It is time to use sober thinking with your next decisions and to remain thinking sober for your now life; it is okay to prepare for the future also, but remember to live soberly in the now, because the decisions that you make right now, will affect your present, future and past, because today is where you build your past, as even what you just read is in the past and yet may affect your now. So make today a sober thinking and good decision making day and then tomorrow you will have had some good in your past, even though it is just one day, which is still a good start.

Sober thinking, unlike thinking sober, requires more than just making decisions; it requires good thought out decisions, as thinking about something soberly requires a complete honest rational understanding of what is being decided upon, as well as understanding why the decision that is chosen, is the one that is best for the situation.

In retrospect, sober thinking is mindful thinking and is what you need to be working on if you are going to be moving forward through full recovery and into a positive, good decision making life. So remain mindful and be willing to leave the "poor me" ego thinking self behind, as ego thinking often looks at what is best for the imaginary, irrational, selfish, me thinking mind and it is now time for the rational logical thinking mind to take over.

With sober thinking you will implement changes in your thinking, attitudes and decision making process and will realize that there is no room for your ego, when discussing the true benefits of this rational thinking, as you start using your good sober thinking abilities to eliminate the negative suspicious self-centered thinking of yesterday.

With your new thinking you will have the power to move beyond false feelings of pride and fear, while saying, doing and repeating good positive sober thoughts about yourself, as you start realizing that it takes just as much thought, thinking and power to believe that you cannot do something, as it does to believe that you can do it.

Remember that sober thinking and thinking sober consists of paying attention to your thoughts, while moving beyond feelings, as you work to remain sober minded by the power of your decisions. Your goal will be in moving beyond self doubt into self victory, so keep moving forward, through doubt and fear, even if you feel yourself sliding backwards, keep looking and talking forwards and victory will be yours, as you continue concentrating on the direction you are looking and heading, which is forward.

Remain mindful of this powerful sober thinking when you are moving through any slippery slope of self doubt, because if you give doubt a second thought, it will try to fill your mind with imaginary thinking, as it works on having you believe the things that you cannot do and the false reasons why. So be mindful once you get a hold of your thinking and do not become sucked into letting negative thoughts and feelings tear down your wall of good positive sober thinking and good decision making.

Remember that to get through any of life's storms you just keep moving forward and this is also true of self doubt, which rains on everyone now and again, but keep looking and moving forward and you will end the cycle of negativity, while turning your thoughts towards positive productive decision making, because you are deserving of much more than what the negative behavioral thinking has to offer, so learn to be sober, mindful and careful with all your forward steps.

With this new thinking you will have the power to move beyond feelings and to get in touch with the real you and to understand that others cannot make you feel, or do, things that you choose not to, because you are in control of and responsible for your life, decisions, actions and feelings!

(Day 11b) 1.4#2 study thought. Sober thinking thinking sober

It is time to understand the true benefits of rational sober thinking, which looks at what is best for the person as a whole. It is also time to drop false attitudes, in regards to feelings and beliefs e.g. that is just how life is for me; Life is different for all, because of individual attitudes and choices. In other words it is your decision how you choose to view life and when you see it working against you, it is your view that is against you, not life, and as such it is your thoughts, hurting your thinking.

Throughout sober thinking you will show yourself and others good positive things about you, as you learn that life is about you and that most of what comes your way is manifested through your thoughts and decisions.

Think about the following thinking patterns and the possible outcomes; be sure to add your thoughts while thinking about situations where you may use these different forms of thinking.

A. I choose not to drink, but I can still hang around with others who choose to partake in behaviors that I am quitting?

a1. Ego thinking may say, I do not drink, but I can hang around with the same people, doing the same things, as I am strong enough to resist because I do not want it anymore.

a2. Thinking sober may say; I will not tempt myself by hanging around drinkers, because I know the temptation that is hiding there, so why chance it.

a3. Sober thinking says, I have taken control of my thoughts but I know how easy it is to get caught up in "just one", so why chance the dangerous atmosphere of addiction.

a4. Logic might say that you know how easy it is to become wrapped up in this dangerous addiction game and there is nothing good about being around it, so why not just stay away from it.

B. One drink, or one day, is not going to hurt.

b1. Ego thinking may say, one cannot hurt, I deserve a reward and I want to be part of what's happening and I can quit anytime I want.

b2. Thinking sober may say, I shouldn't, but I can quit again.

b3. Sober thinking says, it is my decision and I choose not to and though alcohol does not have power in my life why let my guard down, because I know that it all starts with one.

b4. Logic may say that it is a mind altering poison and it has ruined more lives than possibly any other substance, so why would anyone even give it a chance.

C. One day at a time or one decision at a time?

c1. Ego thinking may say, that I can change anytime I want to and I will do it tomorrow or after the holiday or?

c2. Thinking sober may say, I can change and live one day at a time and I will tomorrow, as I have messed up today.

c3. Thinking sober says that I know better and the only way for me to live productively is one decision at a time, starting right now with my next decision and I will make it a good one and if I do mess up then I will do better and make the next one better.

c4. Logic may say; I know that I cannot live a whole day at a time, but the time for change must start somewhere and actually the only true thought that I can change is the one I have right now, as my next thought and next decision.

D. Think about what these things mean to you and your life. How do you define/ see ego thinking working in your life? What about sober thinking? Thinking sober? Logical thinking? How do you deal with each in your life?

Ego and drinking thinking are irrational and oppressive and need to be stopped; sober thinking is logical and factual and needs to be continued for a life of positive productive decision making in the now, with each next decision.
How will you ensure that you use your sober thinking with each of your next decisions?

(Day 12) 1.4#3 Sober thinking/ thinking sober

Today you are going to be reviewing some of the thinking changes needed to be able to be productive in your recovery, because remember, if you want your life to be different, than you have to make it different and be willing to hear things differently. You also must be prepared for battle, as your ego and pride are going to try and stand in the way of the changes that you need, as are those who may not believe that you have what it takes, but stay on track with your sober thinking and do not give in to their thinking, as you cannot worry about changing them.

Your goal is to change your life, into a network of sober decisions and you cannot spend time trying to change others thoughts about you. You will concentrate on changing you and if others notice, so be it, as you will see the change and others may or may not fall into place, but either way, your goal is heading forward towards the person that you are becoming.

With your new sober thinking you are going to find that sometimes, the hardest people to forgive, are those that you have wronged, as your ego will try to stand in the way of you being responsible enough to admit that you may have wronged many, and may even turn it around to make it appear as though others have done the wrong and then turned on you.

It is time to start taking responsibility for the wrongs that you have committed, while changing your thinking, as you need to learn to be forgiving of those that cannot be, because this is about you and who you are, so forgive them for the kind of person that you are becoming not because of what they can do, or have done, for you. Others do not have to forgive you for you to forgive them and this is true growth, as forgiveness and kindness has to be unconditional at this point in time.

It is time for you to learn to give without expecting and to realize that you can give yourself more than any other ever could, as you have found your own individual self respect, for yourself. So be responsible towards yourself by treating others properly, even when they do not return the good gesture, as those that truly matter will come around to see you for who you truly are becoming.

(Day 12b) **1.4#3 study thought. Sober thinking thinking sober**

Life change is not a matter of I will forgive you, if you forgive me, it is a matter of I forgive you, because of the person that I am. So if others choose not to forgive you, that is their choice, but you forgive them, because of the person that you are.

Love, respect, forgiveness, kindness etc. are not the two way streets that many falsely believe and when you give something and expect something back; even a thank you, then you are not being giving, you are trading. Do not try to be a trader, be a giver; of forgiveness, kindness and understanding, which has to be unconditional at this point in time.
In other words when you offer anything of yourself and it is appreciated it, that is good and if it is not, it is still good, as you are treating others right because of who you are and the kind of person that you are becoming and that is good.

If someone should talk bad about you and you need to talk about them, find a positive word, this is not an eye for an eye, this is an "I"for an "I", "I will" think better for "I am" maturing and changing. So if someone does not appreciate you, respect that and if someone calls you a name, apologize and admit that they may be right and that you are working towards change.

To reap the benefits of sober thinking you have to drop the attitudes of traditional ego thinking and work on sober thinking abilities; so put your ego to rest and admit that you have done things that you need to forgive and would like to be forgiven for, which you will earn through self respect, while showing yourself good positive things about yourself.

Prepare to remain in control of your next decision and to speak with wisdom, patience and understanding, instead of ego's, emotions and hurt feelings, just because of the kind of person that you are becoming, regardless of the kind of person that you are dealing with. It is you that wants change, is changing and it is your attitude that matters.

(Day 13) **1.5 Choosing your daily attitude**

In preparing for a better today you are going to need some new ways of looking at life. The good news is that the tools that you require are within your reach and ready to help you to become the person that you are capable of becoming. Now is the time to realize how important it is to pay attention to how you start, feel about and handle each day, from the moment you wake up and each moment thereafter.

You should realize that your day does not start after your coffee, when you get to work, after you have had a drink, or when you say so. Your day starts the minute that you become conscious of the world around you; because this is when you start telling your mind how you are going to feel and what kind of attitude you are going to start your new day with.

If you start out your day with an attitude of "oh why can't my life be better, everything's hard on me, I need a drink, or I do not even care to deal with it", there is a chance that your day may not get much better than what you just prophesied.

Now if you are willing to accept the truth and to learn that how you decide to feel about each day is a choice that you get to make, then you may learn the benefit of starting your day by stating how it is the best day of your life and how your life is better with every good decision that you get to make.

It is a decision to feel better every day and once you make this choice you will realize that feeling the way that you feel is a choice, that you make and of everything that this world can take from you, it cannot take your good feeling attitude unless you allow it to, as your feelings are controlled by you and you choose to feel how you want to, in every situation that arises.

Remember that when you live life complaining about how bad things are, then you will probably have plenty of miserable days, with everything working against you and it will not get better, because that is what you decided and created for yourself.

Misery and anger are feelings that you control, they are a choice and your reaction influences your attitude and feelings, which can become socialized and run through your whole day.

Think about this; there are poor people who are happy and rich who are sad, quadriplegics who laugh and millionaires who cry, terminally ill who smile and people with everything that frown all day long, so ask yourself, who has decided their attitudes for them? Could attitude be a decision? Nothing more than a choice on how you decide to feel at any given moment, regardless of what the world is doing or throwing at you?

So if when you awaken you took an attitude other than sliding down poor me life sucks lane, you might find that what you have been telling your mind, regarding how you feel and what you do, has been affecting your daily life, as well as your physical, mental and spiritual health, along with your social life, work life, family, friends and everything else about your world, which makes this change in your daily attitude one of the first and most important things that you need to accomplish.

You cannot keep feeding your mind the same negative garbage and doing the same negative things and feeling and reacting the same negative way and then expect life to be better, in a positive way. You have to break free of the negative self fulfilling prophecies of how bad life is and start working with positive attitudes and realizing that life may be hard, but hard and bad are not the same thing. You may have been dealt a hard life, but that in itself does not make it bad, as bad lives are created through negative thinking and even if you feel that you cannot do anything about a hard life, you can change your thoughts and stop it from being a bad life, just by changing your feelings and reactions into positive productive thought out actions.

Now is the time to start changing, the minute you wake up, before the world has a chance to get a hold of your mind, you have to take hold of it. It is your mind and your thoughts and right at this moment you can decide if your day is going to be intolerable, or if you are going to take control and decide that you will be in control of your mind and mood for the day.

You can decide at any minute that you have another beautiful day to get through, with all its tests, trials and tribulations, but still another good day, regardless of exterior circumstances, because you are now living on the knowledge that you have the power to decide your attitude for the day.

(Day 13b) 1.5 #1 Study thought. Choosing your daily attitude

It is time to realize that deciding to feel happy, or sad, or angry, or mad, or to drink, or not, are all decisions that you can make and must take responsibility for. Remember that just as it is a decision to live a positive or negative lifestyle, it is also a decision on how you will choose to feel each day. So for true recovery you are going to need to choose an attitude of maturity, forgiveness and responsibility, as you learn to not allow others actions to dictate how you will choose to feel today, as it is through the manifestation of your decisions, not others actions that will help you choose your feelings today, which means it is time to move beyond blaming and excuses, because how you feel is your choice and that makes me happy, or sad, or mad or whatever I choose for it to make me feel?

Many times change is hard, especially when eliminating things from your life, or mind, as the ego may feel an unconscious loss even when what one is giving up is for the better, but if you learn how to change a negative thought or behavior, through an exchange for a better thought or behavior, then instead of a loss, there will be a positive gain.

Think about it this way, sometimes, the best way to get rid of an enemy is to turn them into a friend and the best way to get rid of a negative thought is to turn it into a positive one, before it has a chance to take control of your feelings or emotions.

To understand this more clearly think about the things that cause you to become upset or stressed in a moment's notice and as you are doing this, think about the negative feeling that comes with the stressor and think about how you could change your attitude and keep your ego from turning this type of situation into a negative event. e.g. something happens that tugs at your emotions = a negative action >which causes bad feelings > so you move beyond the feeling with a mature positive thought > producing a positive thought and outcome.

Following is an example situation along with the power of self talk and attitude changes that you could use;

How do you react if another driver cuts you off on the highway? I used to get angry, but now I realize it is not my job to police others and I remind myself that it was just a bad move, not a personal threat and it will do no good for me to give my power away by getting mad. So I continue on knowing that controlling my emotions, through my positive mature attitude, will ensure that my day will stay good, through my decision, no matter how bad others drive or act. Even when they are driving to close behind me, that is their space, as I am moving forwards and do not worry so much about what is behind me. This is an attitude that you can choose, or you can go with some ego based attitude and get mad, angry, and ruin your day, their day and possibly cause harm to others; or go to jail, the hospital or the funeral home, all for the sake of your having your poor me, emotional outburst, because "they were wrong" and invaded your ego space, which now calls for your new sober mature forgiving attitude, as it truly is up to you and your decision on how you choose to act and feel.

Practice this new thinking with things that disturb you, such as; if someone says that you drink too much, or that you have been ruining your life, calls you a name, or cuts in front of you in the store, steals from you, lies to you, or whatever hurts your pride. Just add your new mature attitude changes to these ego invasions and see how different you can make your day and life feel, just through your good self talk and decisions to keep your days, positive, happy, sober thinking events, as you are now prepared with good positive thinking, for when one of these situations tries to lift your emotions out of control.

Think about this! Have you ever seen a fire drill, why do you think there would be such a drill?
Maybe so if a negative or harmful situation arose you would be prepared and know how to act in the most appropriate non harmful manner?
So practice your ego drills the same way for the same reason, to teach yourself the benefits of remaining calm, caring, mature and understanding while realizing that others are also allowed to make mistakes and have bad days.

(Day 14) 1.5 #2 Choosing your daily attitude

Today you will be questioning yourself about your chosen attitude; remember that this is your life and you get to choose your attitude, so why not make it one that says, I am happy, just because it is my decision to be and outside of all that is going on and all that the world may try to take from me, or force on me, the one thing that I can remain in control of is my attitude, as I decide which feelings I choose to feel today.

It is time to realize that feelings and attitudes are not forces that get put into you by others, as others cannot cause you to feel anything that you choose not to, which means that it is you that allows yourself to feel these feelings, so though you may blame others for things that you did not want to see, hear or do; your attitudes and feelings are still your decisions and your responsibility.

With this new thinking you will start making responsible decisions about life, while forgiving your past feelings and remembering that you are a person that can be healed, through personal self-recovery and Comeback Power, if you are willing to create an attitude of forgiveness towards yourself and others and become willing to continue making good decisions, while maintaining a responsible attitudes towards life change.

You do harness the power of change and of a better life, through your reasoning and your decision making ability and it is time that you understand how important it is for you to choose your attitude the minute you start your day.

It is time to stop using excuses on why your day should be bad, why you feel bad and what you wish you had, because it is just as easy to decide to feel happy on a hard day, as it is to be grumpy on a good day. You may say yeah, but there are no good days and as long as you look at them like that, there never will be.

You have got to get this down, you must learn to live beyond your feelings, as they are not meant to control your life, as you are meant to control them to make yourself feel whatever you choose to feel, so why not choose to feel good and happy today.

You need to start your day stating how great of a day that it is and how your life is better with every good decision, of every day, because of your decision for it to be better every day and once you make the choice to be happy, then you are going to be happy, because this is something that you own and decide on, it is yours and of everything that this world can take from you, it cannot have your happiness, unless you give it up.

Most of life is lived in the thoughts, which means that when you tell yourself that it is going to be a good day, this has nothing to do with how you feel, or the weather, or work, or things that may or may not happen. It can be a good feeling day in your inner thoughts and feelings, no matter what is happening in the outer world, because outer circumstances do not have to control your inner world; your thoughts do, so change your thoughts and change your day, every day. It is your mind and right at this moment you can decide if your day is going to be just another one of those days, or if you are going to take control and decide that you will control your attitude and make it another one of those good days through your good mature decision.

Remember, happiness is a personal decision and that you do not have to be happy with every experience in life to decide to be happy, but you do have to make the decision yourself. You can choose to feel a contentedness inside that says, times may be tough, life may be hard, but I know that with a good attitude and good decisions, that I can be the person that I choose to be, aside from anything that anyone else says or thinks, as it is my decision how I feel today.

Choose to love yourself and to feel happy, just because you have the right to, no matter what is happening in your world at this moment. Remember that if you choose to think and feel good today, than you cannot feel bad at the same time, because feeling good is a continuum that you for the most part are in control of. At one end is the low feeling of I am okay and at the other end is a feeling of awe inspiring excellence, with the key being that life is good, just on different levels and once you learn to start each day on this continuum, you will find that your positive self talk is the key and your feelings are in your control and the more of your thoughts that you take control of, the more in control of your life you will become.

(Day 14b) 1.5 #2 study thought. Choosing your daily attitude

Study an example of daily life and see how you could change your day on the continuum of contentedness.

Fill in the blanks by choosing a thought from the list with a corresponding letter and then think of what you believe these examples could be showing you.

I am awake and it is time to start another (A) _____day, so

I will (B) _____out of bed (C) _____and I will (D)

_____as I start to realize that this day will be (E) _____

(A) Great, fantastic, god awful, drunk, trashy, cranky, best day ever.
(B) Hop, dance my way, get, crawl, drag my butt, try to get.
(C) Slowly, singing, praying, complaining, because I have to.
(D) Be thankful for a beautiful day, get ready for a full day, holler at everyone to leave me alone, wish I was dead, go through the motions.
(E) Great, good, a disaster, another bad day, a drunken day, what I decide to make it, the best day of my life.

Hopefully you see the point here, as the minute you start your day you start your self-fulfilling life walk and you get to fill in the blanks on how you are going to feel, from the minute you wake up and all through the day; every minute of every day, which means that it is time to start taking yourself talk, thoughts and affirmations, very seriously.

You should also study and repeat many positive daily affirmations, which could include any or all of the following.

Be sure to continue your daily talk and thoughts with "I" power statements, for your positive change.

Daily "I Power" thoughts

Today is the best day of my life and I am becoming better each moment by my decision: to think, act and feel differently.

I will make better decisions today than I made yesterday starting with my next decision and continuing on, one good decision at a time.

I will start changing my negative thoughts, feelings and emotions into positive thoughts and actions.

I will make my new attitudes, thoughts and self talk, work for me and not allow them to drag me down.

I will avoid negatively charged reactionary thinking.

I will not listen to invalidated hearsay, from or against another.

I will continue eliminating negative thinking from my thoughts and life.

I will be sure to tell myself good things about me often and give myself credit for the good decisions that I am making.

I will make a commitment to start changing negative behaviors by replacing them with positive thoughts.

Today I hold the power over my attitude and I will carry an attitude of forgiveness towards others as well as myself.

I will not give my power of decision away by blaming my feelings on what other people do.

I will love myself today, if I feel like it or not, as I live beyond my feelings and by the good thoughts that I create.

I will not fear change, I will change and change and keep changing, because I have the rights, the wisdom and the courage to change as often as I want.

(Day 15) 1.5 #3 Choosing your daily attitude

Your thoughts for today will be on your willingness to accept the kind of changes needed in your life, to be able to be productive in your full recovery. Remember that you are learning to control your attitudes, feelings, thoughts and moods, to become the mature responsible person that you are capable of becoming and living the full positive productive life that you are capable of living.

You need to realize that many people have overcome great hurdles in life, often involving drugs and alcohol and all the feelings of despair that comes with the thoughts and feelings of addiction. I believed in happiness and believed that it was available to everyone, except for me, as I knew that there was no way out for me, but I was wrong, just as you are, if you feel that you are in too deep, because the road out of despair and addiction is open and available to you, with the deciding factor being on how you are going to make your next decision.

It is time to get a handle on your true abilities, as you think on the things that you can control; like your thoughts, feelings, attitudes and decisions, because you can learn to control each through your power of decision.

As you choose your attitude for the day, remember that attitudes are relative to situations and feelings, which means that you can choose to maintain them as positive and not let them be influenced by the relativity of the situations of the day. In other words, choose to be happy today, before other circumstances take control of your emotions, than you can feel happy by your decision.

With this decision making process, if someone tells you that you look good you can feel happy and if someone says you look bad, you can still feel happy and if someone holds a door for you, you can be happy and if someone cuts you off or ticks you off, you can still feel happy, as it is the feeling that you have chosen to feel, regardless of the outer situation.

What this means is that when you decide to feel happy, you have made a positive decision for yourself and your life and this decision is not based on anything other than your rational thought and because of this, the only way that it can change is if you decide to change it, or allow it to be changed.

(Day 15b) **1.5 #3 study thought. Choosing your daily attitude**

So take control of your attitude for the day before other situations do. This is where your maturity is going to have to be at its best, as almost as sure as you can make your day better through your thoughts and actions; it is going to seem like other things/ people are doing their best to test you to your limits and they may be, but you can always extend your limits.
e.g. you have decided to have a great day; so you get up and it is raining, the roof is leaking, the kids are screaming, you have a flat tire, get cutoff on the road, hit every red light, your late for work, the coffee machines broke and guess what; if you prepared your mind properly, you can still be happy and in control, because your feelings are your decision.
Happiness is not a contingency contract dependent on everything going your way, it is a decision to feel a certain way no matter what happens on the outside and it is your mature decision to stand by it.

Read back through the events above and think about all the negative thoughts and feelings that you could have used and what they may have accomplished or harmed?

Could you be positively charged and prepared for a mess like the previous example? You could if you practice, you could learn to control your attitudes, feelings, thoughts and moods and remain conscious to the fact that these are goals that you will reach not with your physical being, but through your good rational decision making mind.

Think about the things that could cause you to react negatively and how you could take control, by choosing to act positively through careful thought out preparation.

Practice this control throughout the day thinking of situations or persons that may normally cause you to react negatively and think how you could change your feelings and act positively, if you were prepared and got a hold of your thoughts before they interact with your ego, as then you would be prepared to remain in control.

2.0 Traditions, myths and excuses

Some people prefer to go through life, living by feelings, while only knowing, saying and believing what they feel, be it rational or not and they are not open to new truths that go against old teachings. They tend to fear change and hide behind false traditions of "not being able to teach an old dog new tricks", which is why some may find recovery truths a bit harsh, but as an adult it is time to stop the irrational excuses of how feelings, society, the joneses, addiction, alcohol or drugs can control one's thinking, just because it changes ones thinking, but no matter how much a drug changes your thinking your decisions are still your responsibility.

You may "feel" that you are not in control of your life, but you are mistaken, because even if your life feels out of control, this is only a feeling and though you may be doing a bad job at controlling your life, it is still your control, good or bad. If you are doing nothing to control your life, that is also a decision under your control, so you have control of your life whether you feel it, admit it, or not and if you choose not to use this control for good, that is your choice, but now it is time to admit that you have been wrong and need changes in your thinking.

You need to realize that it is okay to admit that you have been wrong. We all have fell victim to mistaken thinking, and have used irrational feelings to avoid admitting that we were wrong, but now the time has come to move beyond ego thinking and false excuses and to be willing to make the decision to change and do what is right, by living beyond these feelings and accepting responsibility and truth into your life. For you to reclaim control of your life, you are going to have to realize that all the excuses have been used up and now they need to be turned into new reasons to not drink, because there are as many reasons for not drinking, as there are for drinking.

It is important to understand the history of your excuse making, because for you to give up this life altering behavior, you should understand everything you can about how it works and how the behavior and lies became socialized into your life. You also need to realize that though your excuse and lies may have hurt other people's feelings, they have more importantly hurt your character, which is much more valuable and much harder to repair than feelings, but it can be done with the proper decisions in your new life.

Now there may be some thoughts here that you do not readily agree with and that is okay, just do not dismiss them, through false beliefs, without at least trying to prove them right, or wrong. Sometimes it is hard to hear things differently than what we want to or have been taught to regard as "normal", especially if those things bruise one's ego, but these new thoughts that you will be concentrating on, are the good truths, which are aimed to help with getting your critical thinking skills working and bringing about the needed changes in your thinking and decision making processes, to get you living beyond the feelings, myths and excuses that have been smothering your mind.

So again, you are not being asked for blind faith, what you are being asked for is to open up your thinking skills and to prove what you hear before you decide to believe it, or dismiss it and especially before you advocate for it.

You will be opening up your mind to hearing things differently than just what is comfortable, common or "normal", as sometimes what is comfortable, common and "normal" may make you feel good, or safe, in your beliefs, but it is time to get beyond letting feelings decide your actions, as feelings often have little to do with logic or truth. You need to realize that you do not have to feel like a winner to be a winner, just as you do not have to feel smart, to be smart, or feel like doing better to do better, or feel like you can handle being sober, to be able to, which is why you will learn to live beyond the feelings, as you do not have to feel like you can handle change, to be able to handle that change.

You should be starting to realize that you will no longer be basing life decisions on feelings, now this does not mean that there is not room in your life for gut feelings, what it means is that you need to remain conscious of the fact that you need to be careful to not create false feelings, that could hinder your life. Learn to understand your feelings, but do not let them rule your life, or your decision making process; learn to live beyond this barrier of "your feelings' and you will go farther in life than what you feel you can.

(Day 16) **2.1 Common vs. normal**

Common is too normal, what knowledge is to wisdom, which among other things is potentially dangerous. You need to realize, that just as knowledge in no way equal's wisdom, common in no way equals normal. What makes this dangerous is when people start interchanging common with "normal", as this is when people start taking it for granted that if something is common, than it can be construed as normal, when in actuality it is complacency, which carries its own hidden dangers that have nothing to do with normal.

You need to be mindful and cautious of these false common/ normal comparisons and to not allow life changing decisions based on the outcomes of them. Do not become complacent in your thinking and be sure to always question that which you are not sure of. Do not ride on society's beliefs without proving them, especially when talking about your life, also remember that it does not matter how many people believe something, because belief does not create truth, truth should create belief. So remain mindful to not become part of a group mindset that is harmfully wrong, as you will be learning new truths about common and normal and you need to be sure that they are not being used interchangeably, or to replace complacency.

One thing for sure is that it is not normal to think that it is okay to experiment with or use harmful substances, just because it is common. Common may say many are doing it, which does not mean that it is safe.

Remember that no one plans on becoming addicted to, or on dying from alcohol or drugs, but the more false truths that we use to justify how common it is, the more acceptable and common addiction and death will become, common yes, normal no, as these drugs are commonly involved in damaging or ending lives and one drink, one night, one more and one party can very easily end a life and yet so many sit back calling drinking normal, because it is common and it is legal so they cower under common complacency, instead of standing on the courage and truth that societies were built upon; before the dangerous, legal, common rights of this poison infected our society.

Stop and think before accepting what is common, and mistaking it with normal and then be sure to be mindful of why you accept it. You know that when many are doing something, that it can become socialized, just as in some countries it is common for children to be killed or used as slaves, but that does not make it normal.

The problem is that when what is supposedly normal, causes harm and yet is still accepted, that is where common and complacency have been mistaken for normal. It is time to realize that it does not matter how common it is, it is not normal to put, or allow the poisons of alcohol and drugs into a child's, a friends, or your own hands, especially when you are not willing to accept the responsibility for the possible addiction, destruction or death, that is attached to that drink and which can be common among all users and it will never be normal to bury someone, due to a behavioral condition that could have been prevented, though it is becoming more common.

In the battle to regain control of normal in life, you are going to have to rely on true knowledge and wisdom and are going to have to come together and realize that alcohol is everybody's business, as it contributes to many common societal and social problems, as well as family, legal and criminal problems and when minors are allowed to drink things only get worse.

Children and persons who act like children need responsible role models, not irresponsible parents, or friends, operating under the criminal guise of "as long as it is done it at home, it's safe". It is time to stand up and be an honest responsible adult, as it will do no good to be anyone's friend if you cannot help protect them, or yourself, or at least not cause further harm.

You will find that there are many places where common and normal are being used interchangeably; which makes them completely unreliable, as what one calls normal can become dangerous for many, as one man's truth becomes another's devastation, so be mindful and careful to not fall victim to any false common and normal complacency's involving alcohol or drugs.

(Day 16b) **2.1 #1 study thought. Common vs. normal**

Think about this common and normal phenomena and how and why your thinking may have changed because of them? Think about why you believe what you believe? Do not be afraid to change your thinking, right now; just like that, if you wish, as this is about finding the truth, not fitting into someone else's common falsehoods and mistakes.

Do you believe that it is common or normal to want to experiment with alcohol or drugs? Why? Do you believe that others feel the way that you do? Why? Do you have any factual proof, or is this just what you choose to believe?

Should drinking a poisonous liquid be considered normal by a logical group of people? Is it normal? Why or why not? Do you think that "well everyone does it" is a responsible answer? Should alcohol be considered a normal part of life? Should it even be legal? Why or why not? If everyone believed it was okay does that make it right? Does being legal make it good?

Do you believe that there is nothing that you can do about alcohols grasp on you? Why? What about on others? Why? Or society? Why not? Do you feel that you cannot change the world? Why? You do change the world with every decision, as you are a part of it and every change in every part changes the whole. Every leaf on a tree changes that tree and not one is more important than the other, each part matters and you and your decisions matter and change the world.

What arguments do you make for the use of something that is destined to cause nothing but harm? What logic would cause you to allow family, friends or yourself to ingest poisons? How about this, you are such a good friend that I want to buy you a volatile, psychoactive, brain changing, ethyl alcohol poisonous drink, to affect your nervous system, brain, organs and oxidize in your liver hopefully without causing any extreme brain, or organ damage, or death because I do love you? Why do you not care for them enough to explain the damages of their societal common right instead of feeding it?

Maybe you do not understand the dangers of alcohol? But, ignorance is no excuse for harming yourself, or another and if another offers to poison you, you can be polite in passing on the offer to harm yourself, while stating that you no longer pour poison into your body and are proud to stand by the truth and your decision, because of the person that you are.

How many compulsive alcohol and drug users do you know and believe there to be? How many people do you think have died and die daily due to alcohol and drugs? How many do you believe would admit that at one time, they thought it was just one harmless choice and that it could not hurt them? How many would rather be sober and alive than have had that one last, or even that one first drink or drug that did hurt?

Think about common beliefs regarding alcohol and how changing your thoughts could change how you feel. Concentrate on getting past the lies that your mind has learned as you retrain your mind to understand why your thoughts and behaviors may be wrong.

Learn to change your thoughts into new truths, while eliminating the need to link alcohol to everything. Think about how you could change your thinking when you think about parties? e.g. Think about good things and a good time, but remember you do not have to link booze or drugs to your thinking, as that's the kind of thinking that you are moving away from.

Try the same with the following: When I see a bar I can think about? When I see alcohol in a store I can think? When I smell beer I can think? When someone asks if I drink I can say?
Keep on working on your good thinking here, while changing what you think into new thoughts with new answers, leading to a new you, that no longer pairs alcohol with life events.
Train your mind to pair good things with the things that you think on and break the alcohol mindset, while living under new thoughts, beliefs and truths and remaining soberly productive and happy, because that will become your new common and normal if you so choose.

(Day 17) **2.1 #2 Common vs. normal**

It has become common and "normal" for parts of society to place the blame of many of its problems on alcohol and drugs, which they do negatively affect many aspects of a society and even though it is society's decision to market the alcohol that causes so many problems, it is still peoples bad choices that causes the problems that the alcohol fuels, including community resources being robbed to pay for the negative destructive practices of those that feel that they have no responsibility towards responsibility, as seen through so many of the self abusive and criminal minded attitudes in regards to the use of dangerous substances.

So yes your actions may be part of society's problems, but that does not make you a problem, just your actions, which can be changed by you.

Society is made up of many kinds of people with many different problems, thoughts and needs and who are seeking to fulfill these needs, by making daily changes in their lives through personal decisions. Now as luck would have it, your condition can be changed through your thinking and by you becoming responsible minded, of which society will also benefit from, but the important thing here is for you and your decision making process to benefit, by your growing into and enjoying a responsible life of full recovery.

Now just because it is legitimate for society to blame alcohol and drugs for many of its problems, you as an individual cannot, because it is your decision to use alcohol that causes your problems and for you to become a part of society's solutions, you have to take responsibility and become part of your life solution by changing your drinking thinking and thoughts, regarding alcohol and all its social myths. So ask yourself how you truly feel about alcohol use, is it good or bad for you, for society, the community, your family, your mind, or body and who is responsible for your decision to drink.

How do others that you know feel about drinking and your excuses for doing it? It is time to realize that you have probably blamed these others for some of your bad decisions, just as they have maybe wrongly blamed you, but be mindful and remember that they too only know and believe what society has trained them to believe and though that does not make it right for them to judge you, just remember that you also bought into false thinking regarding alcohol and just as you had believed what you had heard about how bad and different from others that "alcoholics and addicts" were, that is also what others judging you have been taught; so before judging them, think about how many persons or things that you have falsely blamed for troubles in your life and then be prepared when others start judging you by society's standards, in regards to addiction.

This has become a very common practice in society, basing behavioral knowledge on opinion, hear say, gossip, false beliefs and common knowledge, but you must continue to realize that you are not going to be healed, or lost, by what others feel and say about you, good or bad; as recovery is based on what you say, feel and do for and about yourself. This is why you must learn to love yourself if you feel like it or not and to not live by feelings, but live by good decisions, while realizing that not everyone is going to love you. This may seem hard at first, as up to this point you have not loved yourself enough to protect your mind and body from harsh chemicals and now you must learn how to love and protect yourself, as well as how show others that you are worth loving, because if you cannot show a willingness, then they may figure why should they? As they may also be afraid of being hurt?

Everyone should be loved, but often that is not the case and many times love will not come from where you would expect, which may hurt, but the important thing is that you learn that when you need love, you can give yourself the gift of love and if you need more, than give yourself more. You cannot control another's choices on who, or how, to love, but you are in control of how much you can love, including yourself. You also know that you cannot help someone that does not want to help themselves, so do not display an attitude that you do not care and then expect others to want to help you. You have to prove that you do care about you and your life, by displaying an interest in yourself, no matter what you feel, because your feelings and beliefs do not create truth and the truth is that you and your life are worthwhile, even if they need some work.

(Day 17b) **2.1 #2 study thought. Common vs. normal**

How many people do you need to care about you, for you to learn to care about you? Why?

Your past may have caused many hard feelings and there are those who may not forgive you and who may blame you for many things, as not everyone is going to like, or forgive, you and that is okay, no one is loved by everyone, but you must start liking and loving yourself for the person that you are becoming.

So others are not always going to care about you and this hurts your feelings, but you live beyond your feelings and you are the one that must care; the caring starts with you. So stop the, "well if no one else cares why should I", which could easily say, if you do not care about yourself, why should anybody else?

What is it common for others to think when they see you?
Do they falely see a drunk? An "alcoholic"? An "addict"? A "lost cause"? instead of a person? A friend? Someone who has lost their way and needs a hand up? Do they prefer to not see you at all, due to what you are doing? That is their legal right but that reflects on their person, not yours.

What have you done to validate others negative feelings?
What do you want them to see when they see you? Why?
What can you change about you, to change their view of you?

Remember that you are not living to please others as your happiness should not be dependent on what others say; you cannot control that, but you can control what you say, feel and show yourself to be.

So allow some leeway in others, but the ignorance must end and though others are welcome to their beliefs, you need only answer to yours, which are dependent on factual truths as your beliefs become grounded in truth, not tradition and the truth is that by your decision your life will be changed.

As you put the past behind you and start taking responsibility and living in the now, it is time to admit that it may be your bad decisions that caused or allowed your life to become what it has become? So are you ready to quit blaming others and to start taking responsibility for your thoughts and actions and to change your thinking to honest solution oriented thinking, instead of problem based thinking and blaming?

Think about honest self talk and instead of saying; "The alcohol caused me to ___?" You could be truthful and say it how it is, e.g. I acted stupidly, I made bad decisions, I acted irresponsible and I have no excuse for my actions, but I will take responsibility, be more responsible and will do better.
Now, how will you do better? Why and when will you do better? How will you start showing that you care about life?

Think of the people and things that you have blamed for bad things in your past and what you can do about that now?
Have you blamed alcohol, drugs, drinkers, society, family, friends, jobs or government agencies for what you have allowed your life to become? Why? What do you blame now?

It is important to understand that with a solution oriented life, that there is no room for placing blame, as fault and blame are negative ideas that are placed on past events and you no longer live in the past, so fault and blame have no relevance in a positive productive solution based life, no matter how common it has become for people to place blame for the decisions they themselves made.

You must start recognizing all of life's possibilities that you can accomplish through taking responsibility and control of your life's decisions.

So do not be common, normal or complacent when you can be honest, responsible and your own new person, standing on a solution oriented solid foundation of self truth, self love and self respect.

(Day 18) **2.2 Societies building of addicts**

In pumping up your mind towards full recovery and accepting new ways of looking at life and all that it truly has to offer, as well as taking responsibility for your decisions, good, bad, past and present, you have started a solid foundation for C.P.R. recovery life through a true understanding of your role in reclaiming your sober thinking mind and life.

You are finding that you must stand on your own power, as society's power roles will sometimes build people up through common drinking practices and then turn on them and bill them as "alcoholics and addicts", when in fact they are people who have been lied to and socialized into negative behavioral conditions, through a society that views alcohol as common, normal and acceptable, while allowing its advertising and sale on every street corner and has even allotted the mindset that it is okay to have a drink every day, as long as you do not start drinking every day and as long as you do not become addicted to this highly addictive drug, because if you do, then that same society that befriends the alcohol will "de-friend" you and could label you a social deviate or a diseased "alcoholic" of which you will now be responsible for, because even as they pressed it into your life, it was still by your responsibility and decision to buy in to their product.

It is time to understand society's part in building these troubling conditions, which in no way takes away from your responsibility, but you should be conscious of how alcohol has changed the way societies think, which has, or will, affect you and which gives you the right to stand up and admit that society's problems, with alcohol, should be addressed differently than what they have been in the past.

It is a new day and all of the false arguments for alcohol that have been running rampant through the minds of those who believe it to be a God given, or constitutional right, to supply citizens with a poison that rots them from the inside out, needs to be addressed. It is also time to stop allowing societal misconceptions to guide drinking thinking and to stop conning yourself, or letting others confuse your mind with false or illogical arguments regarding alcohol consumption, e.g. it's legal, which has nothing to do with logical, responsible, or safe and does not offer sensible or mature reasoning. Legal does not mean that it is good, or truthful, or that it is okay to do, legal throws its hands up and says whatever, if you want to harm your life by using this poison, than do it, but legally you will held responsible, so this legal excuse has got to go.

One of the major vehicles of socialization that we all must deal with, is the common, billion dollar alcohol related advertising industry, which has accomplished the task of making it "common and normal" for alcohol to be seen almost everywhere often portraying it to be sophisticated, glamorous and the thing to do, which has also accomplished causing many in society to believe, that it is normal to drink alcohol for almost any reason, logical or not, which is a tragic thing to feed the minds of a society, as there is nothing normal about pouring an addictive mind and body altering poisonous substance down your throat, even if you have been trained by a society that believes that it is the common thing to do and even "normal" for many occasions.

Think about how many references to alcohol that your mind sees in a year's time. Where do you see and hear these references? Television, movies, news, sporting events, billboards, store windows, restaurants, songs, work, school, family, friends, doctor's, President's, movie stars. The point being the same as with self talk, which is the more that you expose your mind to something, the more "normal" it seems to become, or the more complacent the people become, which takes us back to the dangers of complacency being caused by something being so common, that it is mistaken as normal, until people accept it as such.

Now just like you and me, other people also have rights, including the rights to; advertise and free speech, but that does not mean that you become complacent and accept these so called rights as normal, because you still have the right to stand against that which is immoral and harmful to society and it is time to stand up and be heard. Do not allow yourself to be turned into something that you are not, by a society that has been and now expects you to conform to and accept what it has decided to call legal, common or normal in the name of capitalism, regardless of the devastating expense to "we the people, of the people and societies, that alcohol is destroying".

(Day 18b) **2.2 # 1 study thought. Societies building of addicts**

It is time to realize that in giving up addiction thinking, you will be changing thought patterns, as this is not just about quitting using and going on with business, it is about brain changing; which means changing your thinking about common things in life that seem confusing in relation to the societal good and about old ways which may need new changes for the good of the societal mindset as a whole.

Think of some things you may ask in trying to change the societal mindset regarding alcohols common acceptance?
For an example you may ask, is it necessary to plaster alcohol signs all over the community and corner stores, especially in the areas where they have gained such a stronghold. People know what it is and where it is sold, so does it have to litter our community mind, while socializing and tempting adult and children's minds alike, as well as harming those in recovery and offending those who have had others legal drinking harm, or kill; their life's, families and neighborhood values?

Advertisers understand in sight in mind theory and abuse this, based on free speech and advertising rights and this big business maneuver may not seem like a big deal to a complacent people, but for those who truly care, we must recognize that it is our community, our unconscious and our children that they are flooding and "normalizing" these poisons into and we need to care much deeper about that which affects the well being of the citizens of our community makeup, because for every person that they influence to drink, your community life becomes a little less safe for you and your family and that is your concern.

As far as legal rights, that does not equal morally right and there are laws that keep citizens from putting signs up, or displaying what they wish, all in the name of; for the good of the community make up, so would it harm the community makeup to consider peoples moral rights to not have to view advertising of that which harms so many and cost so much, in and to our own communities.

The costs of alcohol abuse on communities is staggering and yet the community must pick up the tab time and time again and it is time for big business to join in the responsibility, not just by cashing in, but in moral responsibility.

Honestly, what good can it do for the community makeup to advertise the poisons that cause so much disharmony, as alcohol has a longstanding involvement in community criminal activity and family disharmony; through divorce, abuse, crime, wasted taxes for civic and legal resources and many other negative actions by those using their legal right to change the way their brain operates, by drinking this brain, mind and body altering poison. This is like slapping community residents in the face with their own hands, as they do not care about the advertising of the booze, that says drink me, as they unwittingly watch community tax dollars eaten up through the problems caused by all the negative behaviors and destruction that this same booze costs the community.

Think about this honestly, because with all the unconscious references to alcohol that your mind sees, speaks and hears in a year's time, do you truly believe that it has no effect on your conscious acts or those of other citizens, which can affect you?

Now even though you cannot avoid alcohols hold on the advertising industry, you can help break its common bonds in the community mindset, as you can change your foundation and beliefs, to not accept that which is wrong.

So even if you do not have the resources to change society, you still can change your routine in regards to the alcohol mindset. It may seem like small change, as it is just a decision, like to frequent businesses that choose not to serve booze, in the name of a dollar; as people do not need booze for a family meal, or to have a good time.

Remember it is not about judging or arguing, it is simply about not condoning complacent drinking thinking. Even these small good decisions show that you care and that you are capable of positive change, so never dismiss the little steps, as every step of a thousand mile journey matters and the steps are ready to be taken and it is up to you to make a difference in your world.

(Day 19) **2.2 #2 Societies building of addicts**

Maybe some things in society have wrongly influenced your thinking; maybe they promised to teach you, or to care for you and instead lied to and harmed you, but in the end the final say to everything that has been allowed into your mind, has been a decision that was made by you, even if it was influenced by strong temptations and lies.

So lose the ego and realize that you may have been lied to, tempted, treated wrongly, or even tricked or forced, but it is time to stand up and realize that sometimes there are forces in society, whose goals are only personal gain, with no real concern on how bad it may make your life, which is why you must realize that sometimes, some people will just not care about you in relation to their own profit. Their world consists of dollar bills, not society's health and there is no real reason to expect that they would care for you and this is no excuse to pass blame, because deep down you know right from wrong and no matter how tempting another may make some things seem, it is your responsibility to understand the consequences of your decisions and behaviors.

Society can put factors into place, to try to get you to believe things and to reinforce negative behaviors as it makes alcohols poisons accessible and can make it tempting, or hand it to you, they can trade you blood for beer, or try to make you believe that you want it, need it and should use it, as they try to convince you that it can help high or low self esteem and that it is for celebrating when you are feeling good, or to drown sorrows when you are feeling bad, for partying when you are young and good health when you are old and then it just needs one last factor to finish filling its bed of lies and without this one all important last factor, the idea of alcohols addiction and destruction will fall into the trash, the most important factor in creating or ending all the dangers of alcohol use, is you and your decision to use it, or to run away from it.

You make the final decision if you will use this product to affect your mind and life, outside of all excuses, because excuses cannot pour drugs into your body, you have to decide to pick it up and drown in it, or pick yourself up and walk away from the deception that lies in the bottle.

It is time to understand that society may influence your decisions, but influence just leads you to look a different direction, or at different choices, but you still have to decide if you will give into and follow that lead or keep your direction.

Following a tempting influence is like walking a dog, it may be out in front pulling you along, by its strong influence, but when you make the decision to change directions, you assert your power and you change directions, so stop being pulled around and start leading your life, as there may not be much you can do in the material world to change some truths, but you can always change your direction, your beliefs and your mind and you can choose to not accept that which is wrong, even when tempting and if you do not feel that you have the resources to change; live beyond the feeling, because you do have the power of change, through your decisions.

If you cannot change something, than stop wasting time and instead of trying to change it, change the way you feel about it, as you can always change the way you think, which means that you do have the power to change things about your life, by changing how you view them.

Do not allow yourself to be turned into something that you are not, by a society that expects you to conform to tradition. It is time for you to realize that traditions, be it family, societal or group are about submitting to another's idea's and have nothing to do with the truth that you will need to start living by, through your good decisions.

So as you can see, the goal is to get outside of tradition start forming sound judgments based on thought out truths, not on what you think you know, or have been told, or is acceptable, or common practice. Do not let ego, tradition and human nature to control your thought and decision making abilities. Be your own person and do not be afraid to stand apart from the crowd, because standing alone on truth beats being buried, with lies, bad decisions and false beliefs.

So, if you can accept that you need educated changes in the way that you think and if you can accept that life, is not as much about you, as it is about the decisions that you make and need to take responsibility for, then you are ready to start becoming the responsible person that you are capable of becoming.

(Day 19b) **2.2 #2 study thought. Societies building of addicts**

It is time to discover some more of your true beliefs, with some "at least it is ?" questions and statements, so that you can see how irrational some excuses can be and how easy they can become embedded into a mind, or a society, when common and normal takes over the logical rational mind.

You will see that it is okay for life to be good, as you learn to be happy with yourself, outside of past negative thinking. Your past decisions may be hiding your happiness from your mind, but once you accept forgiveness from yourself, you will realize that you can be happy, as a joyful heart is not a purchase, gift or reward, it is a decision and it is legal to be happy.

There are many things in life that are legal, that we do not have to agree with, condone, or use as excuses for bad decisions, e.g. alcohol and drinking may be legal, but that is no reason to condone it and just because it is legal is no reason to ingest it, so choose another legal choice, like to not drink.

Continue on with some of your logical/ illogical reasoning.
Drinking out of a toilet is legal, but just like my decision to not drink alcohols poison; I will sit this one out. Remember a legal right, does not mean that something is good, right or harmless.

Swimming in the muck at a leech infested lake may be legal, but I believe just like offers to drink, I will choose to stay dry. Remember that just because it is legal and others may do it, does not mean that it is fun, or will not suck the life out of you.

Many say drinking is "normal" on holidays, but you could celebrate with a decision to stay sober, it may not seem as exciting, as dumping poison down your throat and hoping nothing bad happens, but at least it is a good decision without lies and excuses and one that you can feel good about.

It may be legal and healthy to sell your car and buy a bicycle to get around, but just like that alcohol mind trip, this is a ride that I will not take, because you do not have to exchange good things to do better, but you at least have to want to do better and be willing to make good changes and exchanges by exchanging bad thinking.

But at least it is better than __?, this is just another bad excuse, just as losing a foot is better than losing a leg, but that does not make either one good and this is one of the most overused false relative excuses that you could wear out; as those who use drugs say at least I am not a drunk and the drinker says at least I don't do drugs and the tobacco user says at least I don't smoke pot and the pot smoker, at least I don't do crack and the crack smoker, at least I don't do heroin, who at least isn't a thief, who at least isn't a drunk driver, who at least isn't a murderer, who at least isn't rapist and so on with everyone doing the least, so as to not have to take full responsibility for their own lives and admit to the danger of their vices.

Drinking is normal! Says who? Why would anyone think this? It is not normal, it may be common, is almost always harmful, it touches and affects every organ in your body, so putting something like this into a body may be common for some, but it is not normal, no matter what false beliefs you live by.

Drinking on special occasions is okay, who says? And you believe them? Why? You need to quit the excuses, as every day is special and can be even more special by remaining sober.
But one drink never hurts; do not ever believe this, because one drink often can and does cause harm.

Friends drink, friends die too, I am sure friends do lots of things that you do not and lots of things without you and I am pretty sure that they do not live their live to do the things that you do, so stop showing yourself to be an excuse making follower and become a responsible leader, at least in your own life.

Everyone is doing it; no they are not and even if everyone was doing it, you are not trying to change everyone, you are changing you, so keep your focus on your life and what you do, not on what others do. Any other excuses? Deal with them!

(Day 20) **2.3 Societal programming**

In working through self-recovery you will continue opening up to new ways of thinking as you continue learning how to base thoughts and decisions on new recovery truths and not on other's common and normal, oppressive, societal obligations or programming. You will start today by asking some more questions to show yourself more of where your beliefs stand and to show yourself new changes in your improved thinking process.

So open up your mind, for good positive change, by paying attention to your feelings and thoughts, while allowing society's thinking to stay with society. It is time to make a decision to stop just believing those things that you are told which have no empirical basis and to also be careful to not just pick and choose what you believe, but to seek out proof. The goal is to get you outside of societal norms and beliefs, so that you can form your own judgment, based on recovery truths, not just on what you think you know, or what you have been told is acceptable by others, just because it is legal, common, or accepted as normal.

Think about some of the things that society, family, friends and tradition teaches you about all the places and times that they may consider it common and normal to have a drink. Society will start by making sure that you have the chance to hear and see a hundred thousand references to alcohol by time you are a young adult, you may also hear and come to feel that it is "common or normal" to drink at weddings, holidays, funerals, parties etc. Some will come to believe that drinking is what people do after work, with dinner, to have fun, to curb stress, for health, or to fit in, you will see alcohol at most stores, many restaurants, bowling alleys, as well as carnivals and fairs, beer tents and other special occasions, weddings and holiday events, as well as anywhere else that you can be conned into believing that alcohol was made for that occasion, or that occasion was made for alcohol.

If you drink for all the occasions that you are socialized into believing that it is normal to drink for, then the same persons that socialized you into celebrating will now decide that you have a problem, but the good news is that you can change and the "problem" can be eliminated, once you realize that you are a person with a condition that you are going to work to get rid of, by your decision. You may have fell into a devastating lifestyle involving alcohol or drugs, but you have chosen to not stay there, so now you will work to eliminate them by recognizing that it is through your powers that your life will be changed.

Remember that blaming others for where you are at, will leave you stuck where you are at, as blaming gets you nowhere, as it was by your decision that you drank, no matter who put the alcohol in your hand. I was a compulsive drinker six years before it was legal for me to buy alcohol, which means someone was supplying the building blocks for the bad foundation that I was building for my future, but even as a child I was making lots of other life decisions and this is one that I made wrong, but it was still my decision to drink and now it is by my taking responsibility that I choose to not drink.

Many places may give the drinker an excuse for their behavior by telling them it is not their fault, which right or wrong does not matter, because fault has nothing to do with recovery and you are going to have to forgive the past and concentrate on the now, if you intend on full recovery. So it is time to get beyond blaming and faults, as they will only hinder your recovery.

Now some would have you believe that you have a disease, if you use alcohol or drugs compulsively, which can give you another excuse to add to your mindset, as well as an excuse to not take that important step of acknowledging and admitting that it was your bad decision making, lack of will power, lack of faith, etc. that caused your problems.

So as you move into responsibility for your life, by giving up all the excuses afforded you by society, be sure to remember that your goal is to change your thinking, talk and behaviors and not to convince others that they should believe what you believe, or that what is right for you is right for them. You want your beliefs to work on changing you, not to impose them onto others, so respect their beliefs, as what they do is up to them, do not judge others, it is not your job, taking responsibility for your life, your truths and your beliefs is and changing one life is all that you need to be concentrating on.

(Day 20b) 2.3 #1 study thought. Societal programming

Difficult decisions are something that you learn to be responsible with, while bad decisions are something that you are responsible for, do not confuse these, as difficult does not equal bad, though you can falsely make it feel that way.

Alcohol has an ability to affect your thinking and to make difficult things seem bad; which can make controlling your thoughts harder! What can you do to regain control of bad choices? How could you address these situations, differently?

Whose decision is it for you to drink or use? Can you make the decision to not drink, even if it is hard or difficult? Do you realize that difficult is okay and does not equal bad?

Do you believe that your behaviors are dependent on your power of decision? Could your behaviors be controlled through your powers of decision? Could your behavior become out of control, without your power allowing it out of control? Is not your power, still your power even when it is being used wrong, or in a negative harmful manner? And if not than whose is it that controls your minds decisions and how?

So whose fault is it that you drink? Who makes the decisions on what you do with your life? Is drinking out of your control? Or are you just an uncontrolled drinker? They are not the same thing, as it is still in your control, even when it seems out of control.

It is time to prepare to face "normal", or common, drinking opportunities with new decisions and reasons to not drink.
How can you prepare and what will you do about the thoughts and feelings associated with the so called normal temptations?

Could you decide to no longer consider it normal to drink under the circumstances or excuses that you used to use and adapt those excuses to be used for reasons to not drink?

Think about the situations, places, events and times that you considered it normal or common to drink, as well as of people that you once thought it common to drink with and why you felt some need to drink at these times, or places.

Could you change your thinking, with how you now realize that it is not normal to think that you need to drink at these times, or with these persons, just because it was once common?

One way to end your typical drinking thinking is by thinking about what you will do in place of the drinking?

I once believed that I needed to drink and be part of a crowd that believed they were happy drinking on "special" days, but I decided to change my thinking and no longer think it normal to abuse my health just to fit in with people who do not care about what alcohol was doing to my health, as even one drink causes harm. So now I can truly celebrate with sober friends and family, with having dinner, a movie, cards or? which is a celebration of friendship that you can remember and which you have no reason to add the alcohol mindset to.

It is time to teach your brain that it does not have to link alcohol to life events and you may just find that many more people may agree with you than you think, so do not be afraid to ask friends about doing something different, something without the alcohol.

Break the alcohol mindset and live by your good decisions of not allowing alcohol or society to choose your parties; as every day can be a sober party with sober friends. It will take time and practice before your mind believes it, but you will start learning to believe and you will see good changes in your thinking, so confirm your new thinking and start your celebrating, as you know that you do not need poisonous substances to enjoy a good time.

Remember that life is about what you teach yourself to believe.

(Day 21) **2.3 #2 Societal programming**

It is time to start using all of your positive efforts in the most productive constructive manners that you can find, because your life is now and it is time to start making new positive decisions to recreate it, as of now, to become the person that you are fully capable of becoming. So now under whatever circumstances that you have created for yourself, up to this point in life, it is time for your new thinking to take over and it is time to create a new responsible sober thinking you.

In getting started you must fully realize that when life is hard, that it may take a little more thought, effort and understanding to get a full grasp on your true critical thinking processes, but you can and must maintain this mature responsible stance, through all adversity and do it through your full and capable decision to stand by your new sober thinking, no matter what societal hardships come your way or that try to tear down.

You can be assured that to get the most out of your recovery and new life, that most of your recovery efforts will stay in the now, as we do not advocate for the things that were, or that cannot be changed, such as the past. Now you must concede that it was in the past that you started creating your present and future, one decision at a time and right, wrong or indifferent, like it or not, by your hand or society's, there were many lies and excuses tucked into your unconscious mind that now need to be dealt with and properly disposed of.

So for one of the few trips back down memory lane you are going to step back in time, just for the sake of not leaving out any possible learning opportunity, or leaving any demons in your closet, so to speak, as you spend a short amount of time to work on some then and now issues.

This is one of those spots that you need to understand your full emotional and psychological capabilities and if the past is too difficult for you, do not be afraid to put your visit on hold and consult professional help to find support for the issues that you need to work on. Remember that this is for your whole life, so do not cheat yourself out of whatever it is going to take for you, to accept you, change you and to claim your full recovery, but remain conscious and mindful and never put yourself, or your mind, in a position that it may not be prepared for.

Now you are going to learn that due to "the human condition" you can picture and feel the feelings of situations, without actually having been in the actual situation, in other words you can understand feelings without experiencing the actual trauma, because as humans most of us have felt and understand feelings of despair, anger, loneliness and pain, as well as many other negative and positive feelings.

So to become healed of this behavioral condition that you have wrapped your life up in, it is time that you take some time and look back, but only if it will help you in the now and be sure while looking back that you keep moving forward; make sure to not stop, or to allow your thinking to slip backwards, be very mindful and careful and do not get caught up in the past, or try to remain there, but keep moving forward and be careful to not get turned around.

You must stop using all of the past excuses and myths, including those that society and other programs have to offer, because if you are serious and want to become healed of your bad decision making, than there is no longer room for excuses, you are either going to take responsibility and become a whole person, or you are going to ride the pity party, poor me, powerless, excuse train and keep falling back on how hard it is to be an adult, with adult decisions to make, because there comes a time that you must accept adulthood. Also remember that just as you can understand others, through the human condition, they can also understand you, so stop thinking that your feelings and despair are unique, as they are not. We all have felt pain and despair, maybe for different reasons, but the feeling is the same, bad.

Remember to leave your past in the past, but do not just bury it there, fix it and lose it, to never be found again and when things pop up that you need to take responsibility for, take responsibility for them in the now, do not carry the burden of past thinking forward and refuse to go back to fix it. Do not try to resurrect yesterday, it has taken care of itself and once you take care of your then and now, it will be time to concentrate on the now by concentrating on your next decisions, not your last ones.

(Day 21b) 2.3 #2 study thought. Societal programming

Today you will look at some "then and now situations" where you may have been responsible for some negative behaviors.

Spend some time thinking, as now that your thinking process is maturing you can admit that you have been at fault for some past things and that now you will take responsibility for them, in the now. Pick your situations carefully, be careful to not spend time wallowing in past thoughts; think about them, take care of them in the now and if you start to get caught in the past, stop what you are doing and remember that your goals and life are in the now.

Your then and now list may include the following:

Then: I drank because I needed to ease the pains of life. It was not a choice, it was a need and I could not stop, because I told myself that I could not, which is what I was stuck living with, because of my lack of true knowledge.
Now: I know my needs now, which is to own my decisions and realize that no matter what happens in life, alcohol was not created to cure my ills, it did not help me with good, bad, hard or sad times and usually made things worse, but now I know and take responsibility for the truth, which is I never needed alcohol, it needed me and now it can't have me, or any say in my life and that is not a problem, that is my solution.

Then: I acted as an outcast so that I would not have to be responsible for my decisions, because the so called power of the alcohol was controlling me, so I could not be held responsible because I was sick, I could not hold a job, go back to school, get married and I could not this or that and so on, because I chose to live under these false powers of alcohol.
Now: I take full responsibility for my then behaviors of compulsive drinking, as well as of my powers of decisions in the now, as it is by my decisions that I choose to do good, be responsible, work, go to school,etc. and no matter what I said then, or what any group myths taught me, I was wrong, but that is in the then and I live right now, in the now.

Then: Yes people were wrong for how they treated me, when it was not my fault that I had problems in life.

Now: It was not other peoples fault that they could not understand me, I could not understand me either, and it was not their responsibility to, and who knows what other things they were dealing with, I didn't, I just cared about what I was going through and now I have went through it and have came out of it and now I know how to care about myself.

Then: I lied to everyone about how much I drank, because I did not want them to judge me for being a bad person. I lived trying to show myself to be what others thought I should be.

Now: I realize that I have never been a bad person, as there are very few, if any, bad people, just bad decisions and actions and yes I had done some bad things. So now I do not live life by what others think of me, because I know that they may not change because of what I think of them and they have no more powers in life than I and they have no power over my life or decisions.

Then: I only drank on every special occasion that a society could offer and that gave me an occasion for every minute of every day.

Now: I choose to drink every day, I drink pop, coffee, water and anything else that I want on every occasion, "because it is legal" and now I find an excuse to enjoy all people, while being sober by decision, so that others can also enjoy my company.

Then: It was my decision and it has been done.

Now: It is your decision and it is just beginning.

So keep working your C.P.R. recovery power to the very best of your ability, so that you can see your good critical thinking skills coming into play, as you work through even the simplest thoughts, through your then and now thinking, so that you can become fully involved with your here and now thinking.

(Day 22) **2.4 The power of choice is yours**

Today you will prepare for full recovery through personal responsibility and some new ways of looking at your thinking, so as to be able to learn how to change bad programming and to usher in some well deserved good thoughts through the positive self talk that you will be using in your new productive life.

You must learn to reclaim and control your thoughts, especially those associated with the mood, body and mind altering drugs which have been negatively affecting your chances at a positive productive life. The choice is yours and the decision is yours and you need to make it sober mindedly, as you come to realize that alcohol and drugs will never comfort true life.

So now it is time to take a mature adult stand on life and stop trying to rebuild, rekindle or restore any irrelevant troubled pasts, where new life and new decisions are waiting to be built. You cannot rebuild yesterday, but you can build a better now, for a better today, with hopes of a better tomorrow. This change that you must strive for will be found inside yourself, as it is time for you to take responsibility for your actions and to start using all your power to start getting headed in the right direction according to your life goals and needs.

You are going to have to realize that some of the things that you believe are not be as cut and dry as you once believed and you have to learn to be okay with that and be willing to change, because it is okay to be mistaken, as long as you are open and willing to learn and accept the truth and the fact that you are not infallible, you are human. For an example, some people choose to blame things such as drugs for the trouble in their life and it is time for you to realize that most everyone has access to alcohol or drugs and they have not ruined everyone's life, because having access to something does not cause destruction, now you may say, yeah but they did not use it like I did and I would say exactly, now you understand life, you have to make decisions and choices and be responsible for them, as well as for your decided actions.

It is also time to realize that just as there is no magic liquid that can fix your life, there is also no bottle, needle, or pipe that can grab you and ruin your life, without your involvement. You have to make choices and "well I did not know what it could do" only shows that you made a mistake, as you decided to not be responsible enough to find out if something was dangerous, or could harm you, before you chanced using it, which boils down to a lack of self responsibility, but again is your decision.

Remember that mistakes do not make you a bad person, they make you a person who made a mistake and if that mistake has not killed you, it makes you a person who now needs to take responsibility, admit your mistake and make your next decision to get better by working on getting headed back in the right direction, because mistakes can be stepping stones for the building blocks, of good decisions, that you will be using to move you through C.P.R. recovery.

To accomplish forward responsibility you must take your ego and attitude out of the equation and not be threatened, or afraid, to be told that you headed the wrong direction and even though it may be hard and costly to change directions, change is possible and it is a must and you always have the ability and choice of change, through your next decision.

Think about this, if you were on vacation and you found out that you had driven a thousand miles in the wrong direction, which you sort of have, would you keep driving that same direction, 23000 more miles around the earth to get back home, just because another said you should be careful of radical change, or would you adjust your ego, admit that you did it wrong, forgive yourself and change your direction, even if you had to make the decision to drive that thousand miles back and then start over again, heading in the right direction, with the key being that it did not matter that it took longer than you had thought or planned, it only mattered that you were willing to change and start heading in the right direction.

It is time to stop being led down the wrong roads to recovery which forget to teach you how to use your power and your decisions for the change that you need. I personally changed direction many times, from alcohol dependency, to alcohol and program dependency, to self dependency, to no dependency, to C.P.R. and community interdependence and you must change until you find what works for you.

(Day 22b) **2.4 #1 study thought. The power of choice is yours**

Your greatest tool is the one that you need to pay the most attention to and that is the under credited, very powerful life changing self talk. It is time to understand that everything that you say to yourself has the capability of becoming hidden in your unconscious, where it can affect your life, thoughts and decisions, without you realizing that you are operating from some possibly irrational thoughts that you have fed your brain.

Remember that you have taken in lots of hearsay and false knowledge and it is time to trade these for new found truths, as you realize that to be able to change your thinking, you will need to admit where you need change and then change.

It is important to pay attention to the things that you say to yourself and to change some thoughts on the things that you may have been raised to believe. So how many falsely learned thoughts can you think of that you may need to change your thinking on?

Following are some examples that I have used and heard, which many do not realize the implications of, as this self talk does affect the mind, especially when you add in the fact that while using these thoughts, that your mind may already be confused and now hearing these things, your unconscious mind may not be able to sort out the truths, realities and illogical, or harmful false talk.

A. Do you choose to not take responsibility to control parts of your life by saying "it has power over me that I cannot control"? Ask yourself honestly, what is it that you are allowing to have power over you? How does it have power? What can it honestly do without you adding its power? How?

So now do you truly believe that it has power, or are you using your power to convince yourself of its false power over your thinking? Who gave it this power? Does it hunt you down or do you hunt it down?

B. What might you call someone who became addicted to caffeine, tobacco, alcohol, drugs etc.? How about the same thing that you would call that same person if they were addicted to life, or anything else, "a person", maybe with a behavioral condition or a habit, but a person first and foremost, with all the rights thereof. Even when talking about oneself, you need to realize that you are not an addicted person, you are a person suffering with an addiction. This is a very important truth to understand as this is how you learn to separate the person from the deed and respect the person, even when condemning the deed. So you learn to not condemn the person even when you do not condone the action.

C. Do you believe all the things that you have learned and say about drugs supposed power over your life, or are you repeating and believing societal, or addiction thinking? Why?

Think about the supposedly harmless ideas and thoughts that you have fed your mind: e.g. it drank me, sucked me in, I lived in a bottle, it grabbed me, I could not get loose once it got a hold of me, it would not let go. Do you truly believe these "just words"? Not would you like to, but do you truly believe and if so, how did it find you? How did it grab you? What did it hold you with? What do you do when it finds you? Why?

What about it deceived me! What did? How? Are you sure you did not deceive yourself? Or let others deceive you? Who is responsible for your ability of conscious understanding?

Can you see how self talk is such a powerful and potentially helpful or harmful tool in building up or tearing down?

So again think about the things that you say about alcohol, drugs and life and think about how illogical some self talk, excuses and sayings really are and then stop giving these objects power and a soul and remember that every excuse that you choose to use, you do so by your own power and even though material items may influence your thinking, it is still your thinking, your decisions and your responsibility that you are operating under, in other words, your power.

(Day 23) **2.4 #2 The power of choice is yours**

You can always fight back and regain freedom from the wrath that past bad decisions may carry with them, but you must recognize them for what they are, which is past decisions and past errors and then follow through in the now.

So now it is time to look at not just your responsible side, but also to learn to be accepting and forgiving of the side that has falsely learned to pass the blame, shirk responsibility and to let others see a side of you that you had no idea existed, until you fell into it and could not find your way back out, but now you can be assured that you have found a way out, as you become willing to take up your responsibilities and move forward with the good that is waiting within you.

You are going to learn how wrong you could actually be and how it is okay to be mistaken, as well as how ridiculous some of your irrational or illogical thoughts can appear, as you learn and admit that you are the true choice maker, decision holder and the true power force in your life.

Do not worry about fixing all the ridiculous excuses that you illogically rationalized during the addiction thinking mindset, as the important thing is that you have recognized that you were wrong and are now ready to reclaim your life through the power of your decisions, which will be enhanced with some new self assured, self talk.

This is another good place to put your new learning to use, such as living beyond your feelings, because you do not want to let your ego or feelings become involved in places where you need to admit that you were taught and believed wrong. Remember that you do not live by your feelings and that you can admit to being wrong without feeling threatened, betrayed, or listening to any negative ego thoughts. It is okay to have been wrong in a place where you were desperate for help, but now it is time to stand up and accept responsibility through the truth.

So the time has come for you to change your directions and seek out and find the better decision making abilities that you do possess and that are waiting to positively change your life forever. You are the vehicle of change, towards new life through the power of your decisions and once you turn that power of choice into a positive productive attitude, then true positive change will come into your life through your true powers of change.

It is time to use the whole truth and admit that you are responsible for your life and that drinking is a personal decision and always has been, it was a bad decision, that worked to defeat your true purpose and it was the wrong decision, but it was still just a decision and now it is time to forgive your decisions and realize that many have made them, some have just had worse outcomes, but all in all, they are in the past and now you must forgive them, change directions and start living in the now, by concentrating on your next decision.

Be assured that accepting fault shows responsibility, not blame, as blaming is judgmental excuse making where fault acknowledges a mistake and we all have faults that we need to work through. Fault relates to lacking something, of which you can work for, blame is negative shirking of responsibility and has no logical place in your vocabulary, because you will not operate on negatives, blaming or worrying about past faults anymore.

What this also means is that negative learned behaviors, or faults, can be unlearned, but you must first admit to why you taught yourself to believe them, which comes down to trying to place blame and pass responsibility for your decisions. This could be from irresponsibility, embarrassment, or a number of other feelings, but now you have recognized your mistakes and are ready to take responsibility by reclaiming your true life powers, through your good decisions, which can lead to good thoughts, leading into good thinking and then to good living, so keep it all good and that is what it will become.

You need to acknowledge that you will no longer place, accept or exchange blame as a legitimate mode of change, as from now on you will own your decisions and your life and it will be by your decision that you become healed of your bad decision making, as you are now taking responsibility and becoming a whole person by the powers of your good decisions, because the power of choice is yours to decide to use for true change.

(Day 23b) **2.4 #2 study thought. The power of choice is yours**

It is time to stand up and stop blaming other people and things for your behavior choices, as you have the final decision on what you choose to put into your mind and body and if you make wrong decisions, it is still you that made the decision and only you who can change it, after you take responsibility for it.

It is time that you admit how wrong you could be and also how it is okay for you to be mistaken, as long as you are willing to learn how ridiculous some of your irrational illogical thoughts can be.

Think about some of the arguments and ego hits that you take, in the name of blame. Like blaming alcohol for your decision to drink it! But it made me say and do things that I would not normally say or do, if I were not drinking, which says that you made a bad decision choosing to drink it; alcohol always changes brain activity and may lead to doing things that you normally would not do, but it was still your decision to drink.

But I did not know what I was doing, well guess what it is your responsibility to know what you are doing and when you fall down on the job, it is by your decision and even if it's a bad decision, it is still your decision and your responsibility. Now you have already wronged yourself with your actions, do not add to it by trying to pass the blame for your responsibility.

Blaming is usually irrational and about as logical as you filling your car full of booze and blaming the booze for the car not acting like it should, or filling yourself full of booze and blaming the booze for you not acting like you should. It was not the alcohols fault, the alcohol may cause a problem, but the fault is yours?

Your drinking is your responsibility, you know that alcohol changes thinking and actions and many times lives and lifestyles. So if you dump it into your body through your power, then you are responsible for the changes, because you should know what it can do, if you use it.

Many may argue that as long as it is used properly and not abused, than alcohol is not bad, so I would ask what is the proper and moral way to use a mind altering, brain and body destroying drug like alcohol? Not the legal definition, or opinion, or common knowledge, but what do you honestly believe to be a responsible way to use it?

There was a time that you may have lived by and believed what others told you about alcohol, or maybe you needed a place to fit in? Only you know why you used, but now it is time to fit into your true sober thinking life, not into a life of addiction.
So stop blaming life for the way that you act, as you come to realize that the way that you act is to blame for your life! and this can be changed starting with you taking responsibility and control of your next decision and life.

Stop living by what you have heard, even from yourself and start telling yourself through your own self talk the truths that you need to hear, as you train your brain to believe that you control your true thoughts and behavior, including in relation to addiction.

It is time to quit attacking your mind with false knowledge and bad self talk and to stop placing blame for your shortcomings on the outer experiences in life, when it is your inner workings and thoughts that control how you truly feel and what you decide to do about it.

So with your new sober thinking mind can you think about how many objects in life have ever really attacked you, or helped any other object to attack you, or forced you to drink against your will, because it is through ignorance and distorting the real truth that you convince yourself that you have been attacked by things that can in no way have power over you; the decisions are yours to make.

(Day 24) **2.5 Dangers of complacency**

In working for recovery you are going to keep reminding yourself to remain open to change, while putting to rest the old thoughts, bad decisions and complacencies that have hindered your decision making processes. You are also going to use your absolute right as a person to ask questions about things that in any way affect your thoughts and positive productive way of life.

You will become prepared to question thoughts, ideas and programs that affect you and society. You will learn to ask questions to gain knowledge and wisdom and to be able to know that you are acting upon truth and not upon hearsay, or false knowledge, as you remember that believing something has nothing to do with the truth and one of those truths is that you need to be knowledgeable and prepared to do your part in making sure that you, as an individual, a group member and as a community sponsor, along with that community, do not sink underneath a bed of rotten complacency.

You have to learn and understand that complacency involves a typically false and simple self-satisfaction, with an unawareness, or uncaring attitude towards the actual dangers, or deficiencies, that you choose to unwittingly accept, ignore, shake your head at, or choose to become convinced that you cannot do anything about. e.g. Saying that I am okay with that, or it does not bother me, or matter to me and I cannot do anything about it anyways, is a common complacent attitude towards something that you should care about, but you do not feel like using your time, or energy, to help change, so you falsely believe that it is okay the way that it is, or that it has always been that way, which does not constitute being okay.

For true growth and true life it is important to make the decision to break free of all the oppressive bondages and negative traditions of, that is the way it has always been done, that's just the way it always will be, that is what I was told/ taught, that is just the way I am, that is what we believe, I am too old for change and so on.

It may be true that you cannot teach an old dog new tricks, I would not know, but I do know that you are not an old dog, you are a human being with a learning mind, an active will and a next decision and as long as you have brain activity, you can learn new things, no matter how old you are and no matter how long you have done it another way. So no matter how long you have lived inside this complacency, or the bondages of addiction, you are still capable of change and it is never too soon, or too late, for that change, so do not complacently refer to yourself as an old dog, because you are not and that is just another learned negative complacency that you must change.

You can be one of the many mature and courageous ones, who is wise enough to grow and rise above the harmful complacent traditions and wrongly guided thinking, to become the person that you are truly meant to be and not the one that you were trained by society to be, or that you think you are stuck being.

It is time to start paying attention to and ending some of the complacencies that have been built into you, by a society in which you live and you will be starting your focus with those common complacencies that relate to your current life situations and behaviors, including those associated with substance abuse, alcohol addiction and common addiction myths.

You have an obligation to yourself, your family and your community, to not sit back and ignore that which you believe to be other people's problems, or not your concern, or you become part of that problem. Some of the most prominent complacencies to be dealt with, are those that would have you believe that you do not have power and control over your life and decisions, because if you intend on building a responsible life, than you better be ready to take responsibility for your life, using all your powers, as you learn to control your decisions.

We have all become part of this problem, by becoming complacent enough to allow it to happen, even in our own families. "Yeah, but what can I do to help change society"? You can probably do more to help than what you have and more than what you are doing by saying that you cannot do anything. If you plan to live free of the bondages and negative forces that can enslave your mind than you must break free of the lies and become a person, standing upon truth, while becoming your own self sufficient, fully functional member of society.

(Day 24b) 2.5 #1 study thought. Dangers of complacency

Think about some possibly negative ideas, thoughts or traditions that are embedded into your daily life and that you have become accepting of, but that may need some change?

Could you stop accepting that "life is what it is"? And start making it what it should be? Or stop believing that what you are told is always worth repeating? And start only repeating what is worth repeating? Or stop just accepting what happens in society, as facts of life that you cannot change, when you can change it, by changing you?

Could you become responsible enough to stand on your powers and use factual thinking, while making better decisions for your life today, than what you made yesterday?
Are you ready to positively change your life, starting with your productive involvement in your next decisions?

Could you live by the following; I know that life can be better through the power of my thinking, my decisions and my actions and I am ready to work for my Comeback Power attitude and my positive productive personal recovery by understanding the importance of eliminating all negative complacent attitude's that I may harbor, as I will become fully involved in every aspect of my new responsible recovery life, through every one of my next decisions; one decision at a time.

Think about all the harm the following could cause; "You cannot teach an old dog new tricks"? Think about what this saying could say and how you think that some may use it as an excuse for complacency, or laziness? How could this thinking cause harm? Or cheat one out of a new life experiences?

Maybe you cannot teach an old dog new tricks, but you are not an old dog, you are a human being with a mind, so be careful with what you say to yourself, as you can learn new things and no matter how long you have lived inside this complacency, or the bondages of addiction, you are still capable of change and it is never too soon, or too late, for that change.

You need to ask questions to gain knowledge and wisdom and to know that you are acting upon truth and not filling your mind with false "I can't" thoughts, when you truly could if you would put a positive effort forth.

Think about all the things that you supposedly cannot do for whatever reason, or excuse. e.g. I can't quit drinking, I have drank for so long, and so on and then throw them away as these excuses died a long time ago. If you are not going to quit drinking, just say I do not know enough to quit, or if you have become buried under myths and do not know how to quit, just admit it, but stop the illogical garbage talk of how you cannot, and stop acting like just because you have done so much wrong, that you have to keep doing wrong, as that is wrong!

I would bet that whatever age you are that if it was announced that the industry had become contaminated and drinking the booze would now cause AIDS, that you would quit drinking it, but how? As you said that you could not and now it would have more power and many old dogs have been drinking it forever, so how or why would they quit now? Maybe it truly is just a decision by your power, if you admit it or not and maybe you just need some strong motivation, so give it to yourself?

You can teach your mind new life tricks, so stop pretending that you are too old to be able to learn? You need to come to realize that there is just as much responsibility in being set in your ways, as there is in being open to change, as you live in a country that is changing and where you either change for yourself, or society, or you become complacent and stagnant and get left behind in the lies.

Change means that you are still vital and growing and that you are learning new things, to make life better; so you should choose to continually exercise your right and ability to grow, learn and change for the better; right up until the day that you surely and honestly cannot learn anything new in this life, which is the moment that you leave this changing place for good, but until that moment learn, change and thrive.

(Day 25) **2.5 #2 Dangers of complacency**

Remember that complacency involves a simple self-satisfaction with an unawareness, or uncaring attitude, towards some hidden dangers, which you may claim to somewhat accept or ignore, or falsely decide that you cannot do anything about, but remember that just saying that you could live with something, because it does not affect or bother you, is a common complacent attitude towards something that you have falsely convinced yourself that you cannot change.

So now you buy into common complacent negative traditions, or false simple self-satisfactions, so that you can somehow have an excuse to avoid the responsibility for the change that needs to be put into action.

It is time to take notice and to understand these false simple satisfactions, in relation to your own thinking. Do you sit back comfortably thinking that other's negative societal behaviors do not directly affect you. Think about it like this; does saying that you cannot do anything about a situation give you a false sense of a situation not being able to affect you, because you have washed your hands of it? Many people have convinced themselves of this little self satisfaction, I feel that I cannot do anything, or that I have done all that I can, or care to, so I have done my part and now I do not have to concern myself anymore and this is where negative complacent socialization gets its power. I am done and now society will have to take care of itself and its own and the problem is that we are itself and we are its own, as we are society so we have to stop turning our backs on ourselves and the other parts that need taken care of.

A simple self satisfaction can be a way for a person to remain uninvolved, while feeling no responsibility towards something that they may in fact be involved in, if it were not for this easy way out. e.g. I cannot do anything about my life or his/her life or their life etc., so why try, as this is just how life is. This falsely satisfies your mind by convincing it, that this is just the way it is, so there is nothing else that you can or have to do, when there is always plenty that you can do and always will be, until all of society is perfect, in other words, always.

You may tell yourself that you feel fed up with, or tired of trying, or whatever other self taught feelings that you have learned, but remember feeling something does not make something true, though it may make it harder to want to do, but it can still be done. e.g. I am tired of trying to do this or that and I am fed up with this or that and I feel like I am at the end of my rope and cannot do anything about this or that.

So now it is time to search your good decision making skills and continue to affect change, even though you may have to do it being tired, or fed up with, or at the end of your rope with it and even though you do not feel that you can do anymore, you can, because it is time to realize that feeling something does not control your decisions or actions, you do.

You must also realize that complacency can be an individual or group decision, which adds to its dangers, as you can inherit the dangers associated with complacency as you become complacent due to a groups tradition instead of on your own accord. Such as taking on a groups common truths for the beneficial factor of being able to excuse some of the responsibility of the behaviors, by simply saying that the individual caused a problem, instead of admitting that the persons personal decisions, caused the problems. e.g. we cannot help it, because we are "drunks" and we accept that.

Even once you break all the bondages of addiction and find yourself becoming the person that you seek to become, you cannot become complacent to the truths surrounding alcohol and addiction, because eventually in one form or another they will affect your life again, as they will and do affect every aspect of society if you see it, or realize it, or believe it, or not.

You now know that change comes through personal decisions and without good productive decisions, you cannot have good positive change and without this change, you cannot have the growth needed to be productive and to be healed through becoming fully active in your life, as a whole and not sitting complacently by, while thinking that the behaviors only affect those displaying them.

(Day 25b) 2.5 #2 study thought. Dangers of complacency

Do you believe that your choice to drink only harms you?

If your drinking truly only hurt you, then maybe others could learn not to care, figuring that if you do not care about yourself, then why should they? But people do care about you and their community and they know that you are making a decision that puts many in harm's way and people should care about that, which is why as a drinker, your business is not just your business, it is everybody's.

How might your behaviors negatively affect those around you?

How many ways do think alcohol could factor into a community's daily health, while negatively affecting that community as a whole?

How many different societal abuses would you believe that alcohol has played a major factor in such as; child abuse, spousal abuse, self abuse, how about divorces, separations, injuries, accidents and deaths? How many innocent lives do you think these abuses have touched? What could be changed to better protect the innocent?

So what is it that is supposedly so good about allowing the legal sale and use of something that directly affects and causes so many innocent persons in a society to be harmed? Is being legal enough?

As a society, should we not care about our own families more than big businesses legal rights to produce and market this poison? Would you yourself not be willing to rethink one of your legal rights, if it may prevent devastation in families, or save lives, possibly even in your own family?

If you claim to not have known about the destruction, pain and death that alcohol can cause; you now know, but remember even not knowing is just claiming ignorance, which though an excuse, is not legitimate reasoning.

Are you complacent in relation to what happens in your community regarding alcohol and crime factors, outside of your own protective circle? Why?
If it took one of your loved ones lives would you still remain complacent or would you become involved?

Do you recognize that alcohol abuse is such a factor in society's criminal activity, community legal and medical costs, and many other citizen and taxpayer burdens, that it affects all society, including you, even if you do not choose to see it?

Everyone pays for addiction, what do you think alcohol has done to community costs, civic costs, insurance costs etc. and who pays for these. How many ways can you think of that alcohol touches the lives of and costs community citizens?

Complacency turns into its own behavioral condition and people become so tuned in to the negative trait of "minding their own business", or just being accepting and saying that stuff happens, whatever, or hey it is their right, which are all fine excuses until alcohol takes one of their family members or friends lives, which can happen and then is it still their own business what they do about community responsibility.

Do you choose self satisfactions of, what you do not know you cannot do anything about, so you just wear blinders and mind your own business? After all can you change the world?
It is time to recognize your role in society and stop saying "whatever", as it is time to get beyond complacent laziness and to become involved in that which affects the community.
Stop accepting negative behaviors from yourself and others, as well as big business and society, just because another says that they are normal or common behaviors, when in fact they are only allowed out of legal ignorance and complacency.

Think about your simple self satisfactions, in relation to not becoming involved, just because it may cause you to be uncomfortable, or to have to think, or make changes, or because it may cause you to have to go against others beliefs.

3.0 Eliminating negative strongholds

Knowing and understanding that much of life is lived in your thoughts and attitudes, as well as through self talk, ideals and decision making processes makes it a great time to start paying closer attention to your thoughts, attitudes, self talk and decisions, as you pay heed to the fact that everything that you think and say to yourself throughout the day; good and bad alike, does affect your life and it is with this knowledge that you are preparing and teaching your mind how to handle each event of each day.

So learn to think and talk positively and it will come to affect your life positively, and in retrospect, if you choose to think, talk and socialize negatively, with an attitude of life being a hardship, then in actuality your mind will create a hardship and you will reap negativity, from your negativity; so in effect you will reap what you sow, so again change your thinking and thought patterns and you will in effect be able to change your life.

It is very important to understand that your brain is continuously learning and changing and it is now time to change the negative oppressive teachings that have found a way into your unconscious and that have been hindering, if not stealing, your chances at a better life, because good or bad thoughts are up to you and you are in control of what you plant into your mind, which means that you have the capacity to change those thoughts that you choose to live by.

You need to understand that self talk is a direct pipeline to your inner being and unconscious mind and just like a pipeline going into a well, if you run garbage through it, then you fill the well full of trash and that is what will spring forth from it, but if you choose to only allow the good stuff through it, eventually you will clean it up and you will be pleased with what springs forth. So tend the pipeline to your mind as if you were guarding it for your life, because you are and be sure to use your self talk and conscious mind well and pick and choose carefully what you allow to flow into your well of positive self knowledge, be it gold or garbage, because again it will come to affect your daily life, past, present and future.

As you are rebuilding the life that you seek, it is going to be important to be honest with yourself about the things that are going on within and affecting your mind, thoughts, ego, attitudes and everything relating to your inner being and belief system.

It is important to realize that the thoughts and beliefs that have been instilled into your unconscious mind hold more power over your life than what you choose to believe, as the unconscious controls many thoughts, feelings, actions and daily functioning habits and can be the cause of many unforeseen problems, when ignored. So it is time to start paying attention to those thoughts, feelings and attitudes that seem to pop up out of nowhere, because they are coming from within your own programmed unconscious mind and should not be ignored, as they need to be understood, dealt with and disposed of.

Being able to bury and ignore that which negatively affects your daily life is one pitfall of the unconscious mind, as it becomes a hidden storage dump for things that you would rather not deal with, but have not learned how to let go of; so instead of being dealt with and tossed away, these unwanted feelings are locked up inside the unconscious mind, repressed if you will, to be carried around, like the past hidden harmful garbage that it is. The problem here is that these hidden feelings can reappear without warning at anytime, usually in the form of uncontrollable feelings of anxiety, anger, panic and unexplainable behaviors, which can then end up causing bad feelings, bad decisions and overall bad life results. Many times you may not be sure what happened or why, but this does not diminish your responsibility, which is why it is time to discover the hidden thoughts that are hindering your personal recovery and to deal with them and dispose of them properly and then start replacing these negative ideas with positive productive thoughts, so that when negative reactions spring forth, you will be prepared and in control and will meet them head on with your positive power, to be able to make the needed good decisions, one decision at a time.

(Day 26) **3.1 Actions vs. reaction**

Now is the time for you to retake control of your mind and life by taking responsibility for your decisions and reactions as well as putting away imaginary thinking, such as, "I can't", and to move beyond the negative strongholds that may be affecting your decisions.

The time for personal ego satisfactions is over, as you continue to learn to live beyond your feelings and free of the negative attitude of your harmful ego, while keeping preparing your mind for self-recovery and all the good that life truly has to offer. Remember that relatively thinking, life is not good or bad, life just is and you take it from there, as it becomes a compilation of your daily thoughts, actions, reactions and decisions, in terms of your positive life needs.

You have control of your decisions, actions and reactions and because of that you can decide how good, or bad, your life is. You get to feel good, if that is your choice, as well as to stay sober and to be happy for the same reasoning and even if the whole world tells you different, it will still be your decision on how and what you choose to feel. You can be broke and in pain and choose to feel rich and good, even though the pain and being broke may not feel good. The feelings are yours to choose and to control, as you learn to feel good simply because it is your decision to do so, outside of the impending circumstances surrounding life.

You also may react to things in life that are not up to your standards and instead of using good decisions and actions to change, you may falsely think it easier to use reactionary statements, not realizing that your own self talk is filling your well full of garbage, which of course feeds your daily outlook, as you create your own negatively charged self fulfilling prophecy of turning a relatively good existence into negative event.

Make the decision to stop this negative slide down life sucks lane, right now at this exact moment, because you are allowed to change your thinking just that quick if you wish, so do not let the woes of the outer world choose how your inner world views real life; not material life, or my feelings got hurt life, but true mature sober thinking productive life.

Always be sure to credit yourself for your decision to do better, because no book, program, or person, except yourself, can make the decision, or do the work that it takes for your recovery, as your life and thoughts will become good through the powers of your actions, decisions and determination, so do not be afraid to pat yourself on the back and toot your own horn, because nobody else is going to do it for you.

You will be working on understanding the importance of your powers in relation to self control, through controlling your feelings, thoughts, actions, reactions and ego's as you learn how to become in control of those thoughts and feelings that have plagued your unconscious and played such a reactive negative part throughout your conscious and unconscious life, in relation to your behaviors and addiction.

In learning to control your reactions you will need to learn when and how to let people talk through you, not to you as you do not want to internalize another's negative thoughts and you do not want to argue or give your power and control away by becoming upset with mere words. It is up to you how you choose to react when another is telling you things that you do not care to hear. So no matter how unpleasant another's words, demeanor or attitude; make the good decision to not react negatively by acting like they are, or you have then given your power away and allowed them to turn you into that which you do not want to be. So do not allow them to use your power to turn you into them. Do not give your power away that easy and do not let another's words choose your reactions, use your maturity and choose your words and actions carefully, as what another thinks of you is not what you are basing your recovery life on and you have probably already been called more things than you can imagine, in part due to your past behavioral problems and of which you can accept as true ignorance.

You are going to take control of your actions, reactions, decisions and life, as you discover how to make it you that controls your thoughts and actions. You will learn how to stop reactions and to turn them into positive mature actions, because when you react, your strings are being pulled by someone else and you are allowing it to happen and it is time for change by taking that control back.

(Day 26b) 3.1 #1 study thought. Action vs. reaction

Think about the differences in your thinking when you are acting positively during a situation, compared to reacting emotionally through quick temperedness or ego threats?

Who is in control when you choose to act on a situation? How? Who is controlling you when you react? Are you sure? How?

What kinds of feelings do you typically experience when reacting, while your emotions are being manipulated?
Think about the Physiological, Psychological and physical thoughts and feelings that you experience when reacting?
How can you learn to regain control?

When you react, someone else is playing on your emotions, pulling your strings and dictating what you feel, say and do.
How do others manipulate your emotions or pull your strings to get you to react? How might you counteract this emotional manipulation? Could you learn what your reactors are and start controlling your emotions, with positive actions?

Thought out positive action has to do with acting mindfully and responsibly, where as quick tempered emotional reaction stems from the ego misreading, or reacting on an emotion, or feeling, causing the reaction which in turn usually causes regret, remorse and resentment that will have to be dealt with.

Think about the times that you allow yourself to become upset and how simple it could be to stop, think and change your life, just by remaining calm and understanding situations before you add your responses. Once you start deciding on action, instead of reaction, then you start taking control of true life.

Could you take the time to think before just allowing emotional reactions to take control of your mind?

How do you typically respond to those things that you do not like to hear? With positive action, or negative reaction?

How could you prepare yourself to be ready to better address annoying questions? Feelings? People?

How would you respond if someone told you that they thought you drank too much? What if that someone was family? Friend? A stranger? Would your ego be threatened to the point of a quick tempered emotional response, or would you address the concern rationally, with mindful thought?

Think about the different ways that you would react to similar thoughts from different people? Why? e.g. If I said I did not like you, what might you feel? What if others told you they did not like you, say your mom, spouse, a friend, a stranger, someone you like, or do not like?

Think about why with one it would not matter, one may make you mad, from another it may hurt, some you would ignore, cry over others, tell one they may be right, tell another they're wrong, laugh at one, punch the other. So even though they all say the same thing, you act or react differently for each, why?

Could it be that you choose how to feel when you take charge over your emotions and then make decisions based on confident rationality instead of on reactionary feelings?

This is where you see that reactions are very relative and are tied to feelings, emotions and egos and have many factors that change how you feel about and respond to them, as well as seeing that others cannot make you have a feeling that you do not allow, though your emotions can.

So how can you prepare to keep emotions contained, while understanding your feelings and remaining in control? What could you do to act with the same positive thought out manner, in every situation? Is it possible? Could stopping viewing questions or statements, as accusations and personal threats be a good start in changing your reaction?

When you say that someone else made you feel bad, or hurt your feelings, you are mistaken and you need to learn how and why, as though feelings are real, the question is who is responsible for them and are they caused by others or created by you?

(Day 27) **3.1 #2 Actions vs. reaction**

It is time to stand up and take responsibility for your actions and your decisions while learning to not concern yourself with others ways of doing things. Sometimes others business and lives will draw you into their worlds, by inciting emotions or feelings that will work on your reactionary thinking and bring out the worst in you, but this is where you take a deep breath and make a good decision to take responsibility for your actions.

It is also time to take control of not just your conscious thinking, but also of your unconscious imaginary thinking of, I cannot, as you start changing more of the cant's that you used to tell your mind. These cant's will include those that others incite within you such as, I cannot stand when someone else__? You can fill in the blank with any of a number of daily reactors that cause you stress, but the point is that you do not have to like, or bother yourself with what other people do during the day, even when it interacts with your world.

Once you understand how your reactions can be controlled by your mature responsible decisions, you will then learn how to let peoples talk and reactions flow through or past you, to be dealt with without the emotions that incite the negative reactions which you are learning to control. You will learn to not police or internalize other's negative thoughts and not to argue with, or give your power and control away by becoming upset with others for problems that you cannot fix or that just do not matter.

When you choose to react to others negative behaviors by acting like they wish you would, then you have given your power away by allowing them to use their powers of persuasion to turn your feelings into something that fits their need. So do not give your power to another and do not let their words or reactions choose your actions, use your rational reasoning and choose your actions yourself.

You need to learn to stop policing others actions and concentrate on your own good, because if you want to admit it or not, you probably spend more time complaining about others mistakes and bad ways of life than you do paying attention to yours and though you may, or may not realize it, this has to do with your "reaction" mindset.

As you put away imaginary thinking and move beyond the negative strongholds that are affecting your decision making processes you will also find that the time for personal ego satisfactions is over, as you are still learning to live beyond your feelings and without the negative harmful ego attitude, while you continue preparing your mind and life for self-recovery and new ways of looking at life, outside of the stressors of others inappropriate actions.

You will be working on understanding the importance of your powers in relation to the self control that you will be using to control your feelings, thoughts, actions, reactions and ego and how you will learn to become in control of those thoughts and feelings which have plagued your mind and played such a negative reactive part, throughout your conscious and unconscious life, in relation to your behaviors and addiction.

In moving forward you will learn how to answer some of the difficult questions that you should be asking yourself, while you are preparing to discover some new truths about you, your thinking and your new life of responsible actions. Now is the time for positive action and more responsible decisions and to find the truths that you are going to use to advance your Comeback Power and self recovery.

In working on understanding your action vs. reaction phenomena you can make some good changes in your thinking and behaviors by practicing how to replace the often negative reactions with positive thought out actions and using them in your daily life along with your C.P.R.. Be assured that practicing daily possibilities with your action/ reaction thinking will enhance your critical thinking skills, while also positively affecting your good decision making processes.

Think about and work on your daily action skills, while leaving the reacting to those who have not built their social skills enough to understand that we all make mistakes, which we may quick temperedly blame others for and now it is time to grow beyond the emotional reactions and practice controlling positive mature thought out actions.

(Day 27b) **3.1 #2 study thought. Action vs. reaction**

How might you typically act or react in the following situations: Remember here that you are not fixing a drug problem; you are fixing a thinking and behavior condition.

A: If you felt that someone wronged you according to your thoughts, such as, cut you off in traffic and hollered at you like you did wrong? As a reactionary, addiction thinking, immature or dangerous person, you may ___? (holler out, gesture, cuss and act like the out of control one, possibly causing damage, harm, rage and death or at the least causing oneself much unneeded stress). Or you could take a breath, think a moment, calm down and choose an age appropriate act once the emotions subsided, so how could you act instead of reacting?

How might you practice acting, so that if a similar emotion extracting situation came along you could be prepared with an appropriate action and able to stay in control of your emotions?

Think about it, someone was not paying attention, made a mistake, or purposeful act; you have probably done the same and as long as you do not look at it as a personal threat, it does not have to be a problem, so forgive it, and get over it, which reinforces your power for the next stressor.

B: What if someone says that you drink too much?
A reacting person may react with; how would you know and who do you think you are, I only drink when I want and most drink more than me, or haven't had a life like mine, don't worry about what I do, worry about your own problems.
How might you practice acting, so that if this situation comes along you will be able to remain calm and in control? e.g. you could agree and thank them for noticing, because you have put yourself in a rut and should be glad to know that they care?
Remember that you are teaching your mind to think differently so that you do not react on emotional ego threats, even if a person is trying to be harmful, which you do not have to allow into your mind, as your goal is to change all your thinking, going in and out.

C: What about when someone hollers at you, or treats you badly. Some uncontrolled person may react by hollering back, treat them badly, try to make them feel bad for making you feel bad, an eye for an eye, but how might you practice acting so that if the situation came along, you would be able to remain in control? You might say everyone has a right to their opinion and it would do no good to act like them, so you may apologize and excuse yourself, because you do not need to be part of other's negative events.

You must learn how to catch and control your emotional triggers and you are headed in the right direction by identifying them and using your good decision making skills, to catch them, control them and change them, so keep practicing in your mind, on how you could act, while changing your thoughts and feelings, instead of reacting.

Practice controlling emotions, and learning to not make any decisions when your emotions are running high, also practice some key words that remind you of calmness and to keep your emotions under control e.g. This is the best day of my life, just be happy, I'm okay with that, God loves me, I am an adult etc.

Work on changing thoughts, feelings and people that trigger thoughts, or feelings, or that make you feel like entertaining negative behaviors, also learn ways to say no to offers to partake in negative behaviors, know your trigger points and add calming key words to them for quick association with being okay and to remind you not to react until your emotions diminish.

How you choose to handle life situations is up to you and if you want to be in control, then you need to take control of your emotions and the only way to do this is to keep practicing and to quit taking others words, actions and questions, as personal threats, because even if they are meant to be personal threats, you still do not have to internalize them as such. How someone says and means something is up to them, but how you take it and act upon it is up to you, so be prepared to play the right positive productive mature part, as it is your choice.

(Day 28) **3.2 Eliminating negative forces**

You must learn to keep questioning the thoughts of those people and programs, which seem to have so many opinions about how you should live your life, in relation to their ideals and ideas about addiction, when it is you who holds the keys to the power that it will take for you to eliminate addiction and live life successfully. You will be seeking to live life after recovery and will not settle for living life in recovery, while pretending to control addiction, as there is no need to use your powers trying to control something that you can eliminate.

Remember that you are not seeking a path of false knowledge and broken truths; you are seeking a path of full recovery and of personal wisdom, to be able live free from all the behavioral problems, demons and fears of addiction; just like the many others who have successfully eliminated these strongholds, through the stronger personal decisions and ability to take responsibility for their lives, without having to give away any part of themselves, outside of the negative addictive thinking parts.

To accomplish this goal of life after recovery and not just trying to become functional through addiction, you will continue learning how this compulsiveness is no more than a behavioral condition; it is not an all-defining human trait and it is not who or what you are, or will be, as you were not born this way, made this way or built to be this way.

This compulsive behavior is something that you taught yourself over time, as you changed your thinking, thoughts and behaviors, which means that you have shown an ability to change and now you simply must change again, by changing your thoughts and behaviors associated with the addiction, because with compulsive behaviors, e.g. drunkenness, once the thoughts, condition and behaviors are changed, then by default the person's life is changed.

If a drinker stops the behavior of drinking than the behavior no longer exists, so the condition no longer exists and the person is changed and that is about as scientific as it gets, you choose to change, or to stay the same.

If you choose to live sober, than you cannot hang out with those who do not want to. So if you want to stop drinking, or doing drugs, than do not spend your days hanging around with drinkers and drug users and if you do not want to live a negative life feeling sorry for yourself, than do not hang around with negative people who are not willing to change.

If you want to feel positive then start talking more positive and hanging out where more positive people are. If you wanted to find people who were willing to understand you as a viable person, would you think you would be better off in a room full of drinkers, or a community oriented social function?

You do not need to seek out and find people who have similar problems that you cannot fix, or that spend their time telling you that you have a problem that cannot be fixed. You know that you have a problem and you know that it is your bad decision making, so now you need to be around people that can model positive living and confident decision making behaviors. You need to be understood by those that truly care about and that can possibly help you, the individual and the real person, to learn to live positive and to advance your life, not to reinforce you in a negative manner by reinforcing your past deeds.

It is time to think on your own and if you want change in your life than start changing, change your thinking, your mind, your decisions, your negative friends and your outlook, as you are free to change, without having to worry about what others think; this is about you, so stand up in total confidence and make your next decisions count.

Remember that change and wanting change says that I know what I want and it is different now, than it was in the past, even a minute ago is the past and if you need to change what you believed a minute ago, or for the last ten years, than do so, the right to change is yours.

As you are making changes in your normal activities, remember that it is imperative that you remember that much of your life is lived in your thoughts, feelings and decisions, which are often made emotionally or quickly and without understanding true consequences and this is where the change in thinking and living are needed the most, so be sure to think about your thinking.

(Day 28b) **3.2 #1 study thought. Eliminating negative forces**

Would it help you to have groups of troubled people telling you that you have a troubled life? Do you believe that hanging around with people who do not want to learn to take responsibility for their bad decisions can help you? Why?

Do you hang around people that may hinder your chances at a positive recovery in any way? Why? Why must you change this? How will you change this? When will you change this?

How might it be better for you to be around people who can show you how to live a more productive responsible life? What do you want to learn? How will you accomplish this?

What will you do to start changing negative oppressive relationships? Friendships? When will you start? How?

Do you think that people must hit bottom before changing directions; even though it is a decision that can be made at anytime. You must decide not to live feeling sorry for yourself and to quit hanging around with negative people who talk, act, live like, or think that they, or you, are losers that are stuck living this way.

Do you need to be loved by those who cannot control their own lives and who will only accept you as a dysfunctional person? Why? Or do you want to be understood by people who are willing to see you as a person, who is working some tough positive steps to become a responsible person?

How will you start talking more positive and socializing with more positive productive people? What do you want this to accomplish?

Do you believe that being around positive productive people who can model good confident decision making behaviors could help you to learn how to live life more productively?

Remember that life, positive or negative, is dependent on your thoughts and behaviors and you choose how you will feel and act, so if you want to stop negative behaviors, you need to not spend your days hanging around with negative people.

Do you display negative thoughts and behaviors? Where do these come from and why do you use them? Have you socialized them into your normal daily thinking? How?

Do you drink more around those who drink? Cuss more around those who cuss? Smoke more, complain more etc. around those who also do these things? Does this tell you anything about common socialization? Or give you any thoughts on how to get away from these types of behaviors?

Of your behaviors how many involve drinking for certain occasions? Do you think that everyone should drink for those reasons? Why? Does that include those that you love and respect, would you want to see them acting like you do, in relation to alcohol or drugs? Why or why not?

Do your family and friends feel that it is okay to drink for the same reasons that you do? Why or why not?

What makes using alcohol or drugs okay for you? Because it is legal? Because you are old enough? Because you are an adult? It is a free will choice? Because you have it bad? Or anything else that you can con your mind into believing?

What do you honestly know that makes you so different that you would try to justify this negative behavior as being okay? And if you do not think that it is okay than why do you try to justify it at all?

So how do you think it makes others feel to see you treat yourself in a manner that is so inconsistent with how you, or anyone else should be treated by anyone, especially by oneself?

(Day 29) **3.2 #2 Eliminating negative forces**

Some would argue that eliminating negative behaviors is easier said than done and they would be right, as life is not meant to be easy. Life is about choices, it is about thinking and becoming responsible enough to make the right decisions and to teach you to take responsibility and make amends for your wrong choices.

Many times it is hard to do what is best or right, but no matter how hard it is, you have the free will to make the right, or wrong decision, such as to drink or not to drink; there is a question involved and you have the answer and you must accept responsibility for that answer. So now if you are ready to eliminate negative behaviors from your life, than you must be willing to change many things about your present life, it is that simple, change requires change. So step up and accept the responsibility and a chance to change your life, change your thinking, change your mind, change your decisions, change your negative friends, change your outlook, this is all about you, so stand up in total confidence and make your total life changes count.

As you are making changes in your activities, you do not have to give up friends who drink, just those who want you to and then let others know that you are making a new life decision to make some positive life changes. Let them know that you would appreciate their support, because you know that true friends care about you and what you want for your life, not just your drinking life. It is also time to start planning to share time with those persons who deserve your trust and respect, not those who want it for negative drinking purposes, because you cannot learn how to live sober, staying tied down to people who do not want to live sober.

Remember that just because someone calls someone "a friend", that does not mean that they are the kind of friend that would want to see another give up a behavioral condition. Some of these people that you call friends are lacking in what it takes to be a true caring friend, as they do not seem to mind seeing you harm yourself and there are just too many friends out there, that you have not met yet, who would want to see you sober, happy and productive.

Think about the groups and persons that you call friends and the activities that you do together, if drinking is your primary activity then you should evaluate what these persons feel about you, not the you that is willing to drink with them, but the real you. Are they up to socializing where no alcohol is involved, or do they prefer the drinking you?

It is important to understand that you are not the same person when you are drinking, as you are when you are sober and that all those people that say that you change and that do not want to be around you when you are drinking, are not lying to you, when you poison your mind, it changes your thought processes and you are a different person and by no means any better, though it may make others who have troubles to hide to want you to be around, as then the shadow of negativity shines on you, which makes them not look so bad.

You have to get it through your mind that you are a responsible individual and no matter what your friends, or any group, or the whole world does, it has no bearing on the fact that you still hold the responsibility towards and for your life. What everyone else is doing has no bearing on the fact that you pay the price for your behaviors and it is time to step up and do what is best for you and what you truly want to do for yourself and stop trying to be part of a group of false friendships. We all need friends but we need friends who care about what is best for us and that has to start with you caring enough about yourself to stand up and make the changes in your list of friends, to only allow those that have your best interests in mind.

I have known many life's of the party, who if they had a choice today would now like to be alive for the life party, but that will not happen, as the dangers of alcohol and drugs found them before they found the dangers of their behaviors and that they could have learned to eliminate them through some good decision making and new friends, but now instead of eliminating the addiction from their life, life was eliminated from them by the addiction.

Now this does not have to happen to you this way, because you have choices and they may not make you the life of the party, but they may keep you alive, for the party.

(Day 29b) **3.2 #2 study thought. Eliminating negative forces**

In working towards change, you need to concentrate on all that you can do to implement this change, as you start replacing negative thoughts, feelings, ideas, friends and behaviors with new positive, actions, thoughts, ideas, behaviors and friends.

Be advised that you will not just be eliminating bad things from your life; what you are doing is changing and replacing negative behaviors and activities with positive productive thoughts and behaviors, so you will still have choices and behaviors, but now you will have them working for you, instead of against you.

It is time to become more involved with your good life and to think of new ways to find networks of new friends, as well as new activities to enjoy with the friends that you already have.

Think of things that you can do to find new activities, as well as new friends to do them with, while also working on your "to do lists" of the good things that you have been putting off.

Think of the time that you would spend on drinking, what good could you do with that time? Remember that this is not a could've, should've game; that is past and you are not concerned with what you could've done, as you are working on what can you do now, as you now live in the now.

For ideas on new activities look at the people around you, what kind of things do they do? Ask others for ideas, or ask if you can join in with their activities? Read the phone book, look at what kinds of groups, clubs, activities and things go on around town, check out local papers, churches, libraries, community centers, educational institutions, health clubs, community colleges, internet, volunteer opportunities, as there are many who need your help; you are needed, but it is your job to find out where. There is a vast array of things going on out there to bring community members together and you do not have to be educated, religious, healthy or special to join, educational, church, social or most any groups.

I will not advocate for or against internet groups, as you need to be very careful interacting where criminals lay in wait, be careful with the unknown, which is what is at the other end of that internet connection. You can use the internet to find ideas and to search out local happenings and new things to do, as well as finding more education on what interests you, but do not ever give out personal information to anyone, no matter how legitimate they seem and do not meet with strangers.

Make your new ideas, activities and to do list, as wide open as you can, add short and long term goals, just do not add anything that is unfeasible or which cannot be done. This is a list of possibilities and should be a total win-win situation, so keep it easy and simple. Set yourself up to succeed and you will succeed, but set yourself up for failure and you will fail.

As you are working on your list, do not forget that you already have one set of social networks close by, which you are not looking to replace; you are just looking to expand.
So do not forget those that you already have in your circle, though you may need to reassure, reconfirm or find them again. Whatever the case, you need to inform those in your network of your new found self responsibilities.

Think about these people that you have dealt with and would like to keep in your network and again let them know that though your past has been a bit bumpy that you are working on some positive life changes, through recognizing your mistakes and that you would like their support.

Take ownership of your thoughts and decisions and be willing to stand up and implement change with a positive attitude and many positive affirmations, for and about yourself; including how well you are doing, how it is your decision to do well, how good the change is and how all this is going to help you to become the person that you are capable of being.

(Day 30) **3.3 Imaginary thinking**

You need to understand how the imaginary thinking that you have been hearing about affects your life, and to learn how to eliminate it from your thinking. This thinking has to do with invalidated or unfounded beliefs, often times to unconsciously shun responsibility, or relay thoughts with no solid basis or foundation, which often starts with something like "I can't" e.g. I cannot quit drinking because I am an alcoholic, which is imaginary thinking at its most dangerous, as you have trained your mind to believe a thought with the only basis being what you were told and chose to believe.

Think about imaginary thinking in relation to temptation, how many times have you felt tempted to do what you knew was wrong? Now if your mind is telling you that you should not do something, then where is the part coming from that is telling you that you want to? Is it not also in the mind? Think about it like this, if a bottle of booze is sitting in front of you and you know that you should not drink it, does it gain some power where it can actually tempt you personally, or is it just a tempting thought? If it is tempting you, then where is the tempting coming from? Is the bottle releasing some magical power? If you were blinded and did not know it was there would you still be tempted by it by it? Or could the tempting "power" be in your imagination? What would happen if you took the item out of your thinking, imagination and mind? What if you changed it from something that was wanted to something that was not wanted, which is the key to temptation, because if an item had tempting power would it not tempt everyone, not just those who wanted it.

Start thinking about how many times that you are tempted to say what can't be done, without even stopping to think if it is actually true that you can't? So could it be that you could, but you did not want to. So then why would you say that you can't, if you may be able to? Give it some serious thought and then think if it may be better if you said it like it is? e.g. I can do that, but I just do not want to right now, quit using can't in place of truth when you do not want to do something, as it is time to prove the powers of imaginary thinking.

Throughout life you will learn about the powers that you can use to take control of these powers of imaginary thinking and the behaviors that they incite, but to get beyond this thinking and carry on with recovery you must learn to stop talking about what you can't do, especially those things that that others have told you that you can't do, as you could cause them to be right, as you cannot take control of your thoughts, mind, or life if you spend life telling yourself that you can't.

Now if you stop the imaginary thinking that you can't do something, just because your imagination tells you so, or because it may be hard and if you start learning how to take responsibility for your past, as well as learning how to make your next decisions to be ones of responsibility, then you will have the tools to move forward, with your full C.P.R. recovery.

Now is the time to keep making responsible decisions and using real truths to advance your recovery and to vigorously work your plans to change your whole life, while remembering that you are a person that can! You can change! You can make a difference! You can be healed and you can make good decisions towards personal self-recovery!

Eliminating imaginary thinking has got to be a priority in eliminating strongholds in your life and to accomplish this life change you will have to continue to move beyond false ego satisfactions.

So how many things have you taught yourself that you cannot do, or cannot do on your own, or by yourself? Or can't do today, or can't do in my condition, or can't do just because. How many of those things that you could not do, have you done, how many do you believe that you could do if you wanted to; so start saying that you can do whatever it is, even if you choose not to, because this is using your positive decision making process, which is much stronger than any negative lie of, I can't. The key here is to know the difference between the truth and the truth according to imaginary thinking as well as half truths, false knowledge, illogical thinking and cant's, because it has become too common to use I can't in place of the truths of, I do not know how, or I do not wish to, or?

(Day 30b) 3.3 #1 study thought. Imaginary thinking

Think about how many times you say what cannot be done, by you or others, without even stopping to think if it is true.
How often do you say that you cannot do something, when you actually could if you tried, or wanted to?

If you choose to not do something, you still made a decision, which is a positive force, even when used in a negative manner, as making a choice to not do something is a stronger statement than any negative statement of I can't.
So own your decision of what you wish to not do and be honest about it; do not just say I cannot, say I choose not to, or do not want to, or have not learned how yet. I do not know how will always beat I cannot.

As you start understanding the hidden powers in this word of can't, you will discover its false powers in relation to your harmful negative imaginary thinking, which in turn may help you to see the power in its counterpart of, yes I can!

How many things have you taught yourself that you can't do, or can't do on your own, or by yourself, or can't do today, or can't do right now, or in my condition, or because? Because of what? How many ways can you think of that you relay; I can't?

"I cannot quit drinking on my own!" sure you can, just as many others who could not, did! Once they started saying, I not only can, I will.

Stop telling yourself that you can't do something that you're not sure of, start telling yourself that you can and will and then take control of your life and your decisions. Think about the things that you can do, even if not at this moment, which you falsely state that you can't. I once falsely said that I can't _?, but actually I can't _? under my current circumstances, but there are things that I could change and make it to where I could _?. So even though I cannot do it at this moment, the answer to can I _?, Is yes I can; I just need to put a plan together and this is much more positive, productive and truthful than, I can't.

So can you quit drinking and start living a good life? Sure you can! You just need to put a plan together! Which is a positive, productive and truthful "I can" mindset and is much stronger and more productive than, "I can't".

What other damaging thoughts have you used to hinder your daily life? What about, I don't know, don't care, should have, should not etc. One thing that you can't do here is you cannot get better if you keep feeding on negatives and cants.

Take some time and start telling your mind everything that you can think of that you have learned to do, through your decision to do so and then think about what do you truly mean when you say you can't? Do you just mean that you haven't learned how? Or that you do not have the time, skills or patience? are you lacking something that could make it to where you could?

You are not looking for earth shattering changes here; just to prove to your mind that you have the ability to learn. I have learned to do many things that I thought that I could not do, such as: I learned to walk, when I did not know how and said I can't. I learned to read, when I did not know how and said I can't. I learned to; ride a bike, to drive, to socialize, to make friends, to get drunk, to be a compulsive drinker, to put myself down and now how to live sober. So what do all these things have in common with most live events? Look close and you will see that they are all learned and probably at one time falsely had can't attached to them.

So tell yourself good truths that you are working on learning. e.g. I will stop drinking, because now I have learned how. I will reclaim my good life, because now I am learning how. Keep your list of good, thinking and growing; do not keep good thoughts hidden, keep your mind informed of all that you plan on doing to make life better through your decision making processes and C.P.R.
Keep flooding your mind with good things and there will not be room for all the imaginary cants.

(Day 31) **3.3 #2 Imaginary thinking**

Temptations can at times seem to feel stronger than most any power you could imagine, but there is a key factor that you must pay attention to and understand and it lays within the action words of temptation. The key words come with what temptation does, it seems and it feels and it lies in your mind; beyond that it is all up to you and is your responsibility on how you use your ability to respond to what that temptation makes you feel, or what it seems like it wants you to do.

Temptation brings an "I need it feeling", which is a lie and is imaginary thinking, which you can bypass with your patience and you will find that the more that you stand up and push it away, the weaker it will become, until it dissipates; as without feeding into it there will be no reason for it to tempt you. You must remember here that these are feelings and you are learning to live beyond feelings, no matter how strong they appear, because you are also stronger than you appear.

Did you ever wonder how or why so many people are not tempted to drink and not tempted to drown their sorrows or celebrate with a drink? Think about it; why would temptation strike where it is not wanted? These people tell their minds that they do not want to drink and they make the good choice not to; they do not feed temptation and it wanes.

You too can control your feelings and temptations and also not drink because of your decision not to and if you will truly decide not to, there will not be any room for any temptation. So this makes being tempted, imaginary thinking, as it can be overcome with logical thought, which also makes saying "I can't resist it due to its temptation feeling" illogical reasoning, as this is trying to give your power away to a feeling which you must live beyond.

The key with temptation just like with all imaginary thinking is to know the difference between truth, because it is honest logical truth and imaginary truth, including temptations, half truths, falsehoods, ego's, false knowledge and illogical thinking and any other imaginary excuse maker that may enter your thinking, if you are not mindful.

Think about this temptation; the one that you say you cannot stop because it is so strong; so when you are walking through a store and this temptation hits, do you open up a bottle and start drinking? Why not? Yes I know many reasons why not to, but I thought that you could not control temptation? Aren't you controlling it if you do not drink it everywhere? Okay so you can control it when you have to, but then it__? It what? Makes you feel bad? So what! Giving into it is going to make you do bad and probably feel worse.

Have you ever felt like you had to have a drink so bad that you almost felt like you may die if you did not get a drink quick, so you go to the store barely able to make it through line and get outside so that you can get this poison dumped into your system and once outside the temptation is not that strong anymore and you no longer have a dire urgency to open the bottle and you believe it is because at least you have it in your hand, not realizing that you rode out the temptation. So what is this is truly saying about temptation?

You need to think about these cants for a moment, including those in regards to temptations. How many times have you heard someone say that something was too tempting, almost believing that this is a good excuse to give away power?

Temptation just says that something inside you wants it, but something else knows that for some reason it may be wrong. So if you think it may be wrong, than where is the part coming from that is telling you that you want it? It has to be from the same place that gives you the power to resist it.

This takes the good thinking skills that you have been working on, because this temptation battle starts in the mind, is fought in the mind and is won or lost in the mind all in the name of I want, so change your wants, because the temptation starts once you acknowledge your mind telling you that you want something.

Think about it, if your mind, or the thought, was stopped you would not be tempted, because temptations like all thoughts, feelings and emotions are in the mind and can cause you to believe most anything that you are willing to tell yourself to believe, so tell yourself, "I don't get tempted anymore" and enjoy learning to end the temptations in your life.

(Day 31b) **3.3 #2 study thought. Imaginary thinking**

Think about some temptations that you have felt in your life. What do you like, or crave that when you see it, you want it and will start making excuses of why you have to have it. So what do you think will happen if you do not get it? Can you survive without it? Will you feel bad? Can you survive feeling bad? How long do you think that you would feel bad without it? Would you feel bad with it? Do you live according to your feelings? How could you learn to live beyond these feelings? Could you change your feelings?

What if you give into the temptation, what might happen then? Could this reinforce the negative behavior and the temptation?

Where does temptation truly come from? Is it in your mind? Is it created by you to allow yourself to do something that you maybe should not, while giving yourself a false excuse to do it?

Is the power in the object, or in the mind that sees and wants it? If thinking about it makes you want it, than is the temptation in the thought which is in the mind?

Since temptation is in your mind is it controllable by you, since you control your mind?

What do you think about temptation being on a continuum (continu-um) in your mind; where on the right you feel extreme temptation, and on the left you have the, do not want it. Think about it holding your hands out, palms up and in your mind weigh them back and forth, with right hand "I wants", left hand "I do not wants" now think about an imaginary line connecting them, now on this line you can place your wants and needs, realizing that the farther you place them towards the right the more temptation power you give them. e.g. alcohol or drugs may be on the far right, but if you learn to take that power back and move the want more towards the left, you can then get it to the side of no temptation, as your scale ranges from have to have it, into do not want it.

Once you realize that objects do not have tempting power and that the tempting power is coming from your very own mind and once you teach your mind that you no longer like, want, or need an object, then there will be no reason to feel tempted.

Can you see how the more that you push it away, the weaker temptation becomes? What things have you seen this work on?

Ask people who do not drink why they are not tempted and they may not know, except for that they choose not to be and you will find that once you convince yourself that you do not want it, than you will no longer give it tempting power, though now and again your thoughts may slip and think about it, but you do not live by fleeting moments, or feelings.

Think about an item that tempts you, what does it actually do? What do you do? What would happen to the temptation, if you ignored it? Before you say that it is too strong to ignore, think about how you could lessen the thoughts of how tempting it is.

What would happen if you changed this temptation from a feeling of something that is wanted, to something that was unacceptable, in your own mind? e.g. instead of telling yourself how much you want the item and how good it sounds, why not start telling yourself how you do not need, or want, this nasty item in your life.

Define the following and what role they may play in your life, as well as how you may combat against them.

Temptation – what does temptation look or feel like for you? What can you do about it? Can a temptation control your life? Or can you learn to control and eliminate the feeling of temptation?

Imaginary thinking- What can you do to eliminate imaginary thoughts of what you cannot do? Could you look at the positive things that you can do instead of imagining all that you cannot do.

(Day 32) **3.4 No time for ego's**

Now is the time to realize that you can take control of your mind, thoughts and life by taking responsibility for your decisions and just as you learned to put away imaginary thinking, to be able to move beyond negative strongholds, you will also learn that there is no time or room for the personal ego satisfactions that create false feelings of self importance or defeat. Now there is plenty of room for true self importance in your life, because you are important, but you are going to have to understand the difference between ego importance and self importance, as they pertain to self pride, or pride in oneself.

You will have to learn to not become absorbed in the egotistical feelings of false pride and assumed ego threats, as you move forward and continue preparations for self-recovery, self discovery and new ways of looking at life and all the good that it has to offer. You will also need to realize that you may not always know or do what is best, but as long as you keep open to new ideas, while continuing to search for and work towards what is best, while being prepared to learn and discover new truths about you and your life plan, then you will be ready to move forward in your C.P.R. recovery.

Now is the time to start making decisions to find the truths that you are going to use to advance your recovery. You will start by realizing that you can be healed and that this healing will come through your good decisions and personal self-recovery and that it will be through your hard work and your decisions, that your life will be changed for the better, with the only limits on your new life being the ones that you allow to stand in your way.

You will be preparing your thoughts, mind and ego as you work on learning how important it is to not let ego satisfactions control your life. You do harness the power of change and of a better life through your reasoning and your decision making ability and it is time to start putting these powers into action. Remember as you are striving for new life satisfaction that it is by your power that you will reach your goals and you do not want your ego to take control of your power, as right now you need to retain full conscious control of yourself as a whole person.

In preparing your life for no ego satisfactions you are going to need to know how to repair the damages incurred throughout addiction, along with being ready to control any present day feelings, because even though you will no longer live by the false feelings of what you or others have to say, about past bad decisions, these ego bruises usually will not just disappear without being consciously worked through, understood and forgiven, so that they will have no chance to reappear at a later time.

As you are learning to forgive past decision making, it will be good if you are strong enough to look at some of the feelings and thoughts that have hurt your ego, your pride and your feelings, so that you may practice thinking about them in a new way, with a new mindset and new thoughts about them, so as to be able to change their harmful abilities into what they truly are; nothing more than words and feelings that need looked at, turned around and tossed away by your decision and powers of change.

Again, it is important to not live by your feelings, but you still need to know where your feelings came from and how and why they came, as well as how to properly dispose of them. You are going to learn that when others say things about you, or if your ego thinks they are, or if they insinuate things, or point their finger at you, or disagree with you, that what they are doing has to do with their false beliefs, not your truths. So do not give your power away by letting your ego take over, where you can just as easily choose to allow logic to take over and to start replacing any perceived threats with logic, truth, thought and maturity.

There are many things in your past that allowed harmful negative feelings into your unconscious, due to your ego not wanting to dismiss what it interpreted as a threat to one's pride. The key is not if what others said or did was right or wrong, the key is; what did your mind do with it? In other words, if someone said that you were something that you were not, did you become that something, or dismiss the opinion as irrelevant? Remember this is about you, your mind, your decisions and your life and it is time to start using your decisions and powers to control these feelings, as it is you that holds the true power of change.

(Day 32b) **3.4 #1 study thought. No time for ego's**

Life can seem, or feel, punishing at times, if you allow it to feel that way, or it can be full of learning experiences that you can work through and learn from, if you choose to see it that way.
e.g. Think back before you could ride a bike, you may not remember this ego bashing era of thinking, or being told that you could not do something else, but you probably stepped up and through repetition you learned how to do this new task, or not and moved on with life; to start learning how to get past all the other new things where your ego pretended to help, but actually harmed and yet you moved beyond the feelings and thoughts to be able to do all the things that you once could not. You learned to turn your imaginary I can't's, into real life yes I can's, step by step, you did what had to be done.

Think about school and how grades can be punishing, as you try to live up to them, or make excuses for them, to later try to live them down; depending on how good or bad you made yourself feel, because of them. Now you have different experiences to take care of, but they are no more important to your ego now, than learning new things was then.
The important issue here is; does being graded make you feel good or bad, or is it your choice of thoughts that makes, or allows you to feel, good or bad? Could you decide to feel differently and to live beyond the feelings and grading? Could you choose today how to feel when being graded by others? Or do you have to feel how they expect you to feel? Do you realize that the way you choose to view your world and past life events can have a great effect on your now life events?

Did you know that your thoughts will guide your feelings, as to how you feel that others should treat you, but you must realize that others have their own agendas, with their own thoughts; so it is time for you to take your ego out of their equation, as you are learning how to not live by feelings, but by your productive truths; while remembering that what others say, or believe, about you, has no bearing on the person that you are now becoming.

The biggest difference now, in your new learning, is that your mind has the maturity to counteract the ego hits, but just like every other productive process, it has to be in tune with your critical thinking skills and decision making processes, as well as with your willingness to change. This is because to be able to get in touch with and change these ego threats you are going to have to recognize them for what they are and then work to change them. You are going to need to think about and recognize your ego at work, to recognize where the changes in your thoughts will be most productive. So think about your typical day's thoughts, good, bad or indifferent, as you need to be able to recognize the thoughts that can affect your life.

Through your ego and emotions when someone calls you a loser, a drunk, or an addict, it can hurt as it invokes the "name calling" feelings that you learned as a child and have always used, but now it is time to learn to drop this ego thinking, start living beyond the feelings while speaking and seeking positive change.

It is also time to be mindful of the kinds of people that you give this supposed power to make you feel good or bad, to?
Think of the people or things that you typically come into contact with and how you may give them your power, by allowing their words and actions, to manipulate your feelings, thoughts and emotions?

Do others good, bad or ignorant actions upset you? How? Why? Are you in effect receiving or allowing the feelings?
This is important; so study it until you understand it. Other people cannot make you feel anything that you do not for some internal reason choose to feel!
The process starts as someone does something that goes from your eyes, or ears, into your brain and offends your ego, which transfers it to your emotions and can add negativity, which then sends it into your choice of feelings, which can be harmful, as it ships part of it back to your brain, which decides on an action, or reaction to shoot out your mouth, or some other behavior choice. So what happens if it is counteracted, as soon as it hits your eyes or ears, before it affects your ego?

(Day 33) **3.4 #2 No time for ego's (Day 41)**

Egos are another way for others to influence and try to control your thinking, thoughts, decisions and attitudes, which works especially well when there is already an underlying condition, oppressing your thoughts about yourself, such as a negative behavioral condition like substance abuse. Think about how many times someone has told you that you cannot do something and your ego either went into a poor me, I can't do anything state, or jumped up and said I can to do that, I can do anything, you may have even took this attitude on things that you could not do, but did not want to admit to.

What about if a person that you trusted started teaching you that you can't quit drinking, now had you heard it once and let your ego jump in and say oh yes I can and started telling yourself a hundred times a day and believing that, yes you can quit on your own, then you would have a great chance, but once it is pounded into you that you cannot, then your ego may come to accept it as a protective excuse, instead of the personal threat that it is.

So be careful to not give your power away by letting your ego take over where you can just as easily choose to allow your logic to take over, which you are going to find to be a key in getting beyond ego satisfactions, as you learn to start replacing them with logic, truth, thought and maturity.

As you are learning to forgive your past decision making and to be proud of taking responsibility for your new decision making, it is important to compare, contrast, think about and understand, your true feelings, in relation to learned feelings. These differences may consist of responsible thoughts of pride and healthy suspicion towards life situations and self actions, or ego pride and dangerous self doubt, aimed towards invoking quick uncontrolled emotions.

You will find that healthy pride and doubt can come from within and extend out, so you can take pride, but do not become over proud, you can have doubts and use them to learn and for safety, but do not internalize them as suspicious feelings, as you live beyond feelings and by truths.

Look at some of the people, feelings and thoughts that have hurt your ego, pride and feelings and then practice thinking about them in a new way, with a new mindset and new thoughts and new self talk about them, as you are learning how important it is to remember that you do not live by your feelings, your past, or your ego, or others thoughts and feelings; because you live beyond feelings and ego satisfactions, so you are going to learn to start replacing them with logic, truth, thought and maturity, because that is what it will take to positively change your inner world.

Now is also the time to realize that even though there is no time or room for negative or controlling personal ego satisfactions, which work to create false feelings of self importance, or self defeat, that there is plenty of room for honest self importance, good thoughts and true feelings, as well as true emotions, but you are going to have to understand the difference between negative ego satisfactions and true self importance and legitimate positive productive satisfactions, to productively move forward.

It is Important to understand that outside of all the negative emotions that can be created from the ego, that ego's and emotions are not bad things when they are used maturely. We need emotions, as they make us human and we need ego's as that gives us drive to strive to be better, so just like most everything else that you have at your disposal to create the life that you are creating, they can be used for good or bad, positive or negative and it is going to take your critical thinking and good decision making skills to keep them working for you.

Living with no ego satisfactions will not keep you from doing or feeling good, but it will keep you from doing good just in the name of feeling good. Now your motivation instead of recognition will be to do good because of the person that you are and because you choose to do good, not because others recognize you as good. In other words, you're feeling good about yourself will no longer be dependent on how others feel about you. You will feel good about you, simply because you deserve to and because it is your decision to.

(Day 33b) **3.4 #2 study thought. No time for ego's**

Think about some things that have happened, where your ego has possibly taken over your logic, where your mouth may have taken over before your brain had a chance to think?
Could you recognize and change similar situations that arise in these battles between ego and logic?
The key is to avoid the pitfalls that follow ego thinking. Following are a couple of examples; there is no right or wrong, so be sure to take your thinking to where you need it to be, for it to do the most good for you.

Ego thinking says: I drink because I want to! Though I cannot quit because it is not my fault that I drink! It was others that caused the mess that I am living in.
Logic says: It was my decision to drink, I chose foolishly but I can change, as it is my mind and life and I know that no one can quit for me and it may be tough but I can do it, for me.

Ego says: I need to be around people who know addiction thinking, so that I can be part of a group who understands how bad life is on me, I do not need people who have not walked in my shoes, telling me anything about my life.
Logic says: I cannot get better around those who do not know how to live better, or who believe that they are okay being not okay. I need to be with people that live and think differently, even at the risk of being the "odd one". I need to find the wisdom to realize that I am an acceptable interdependent part of society that needs to learn to think differently, by being around people who think differently.

Ego says: Other people just do not understand me, but someday I will show them.
Logic says: Maybe others are not meant to, or do not want to understand me and that's alright. It is time to forget about someday and about showing anyone anything and just work on my next good decisions. I can make good decisions and stick by them and show myself that I do matter, as much as anyone else, as today is the day I can that I can find and understand my true self.

Take some time to think about other situations and what your ego may say and list some logical ideas that you can use to counteract the ego's negative emotions and feelings, so that you can start standing on what logical decision making says.

Ego, feelings, emotions, choices, truths, lies, gossip, etc. all work to influence the minds negative harmful ego satisfactions, so you need to understand what each means to you and how they can influence your life. Now is the time to realize the difference between negative ego satisfactions, true self importance and legitimate positive satisfactions, as it is important to understand that outside of all the negative emotions that can be created from the ego, that ego's and emotions are not necessarily bad when they are understood, controlled and used in their proper context.

You need to acknowledge your feelings, but do not live to have them acknowledged by others, as this could cause disappointment and you do not need to set yourself up to feel bad. Also do not expect others to recognize your good deeds, but keep doing them and keep recognizing yourself for the good person that you are, in other words, take control of your ego by allowing the self importance of being in control of your good decisions to flourish, without needing ego inflations from yourself or others.

Can you think of some positive thoughts or actions that are part of your character, which shows your true self? In other words, those positive productive selfless things that make you feel good without anyone patting you on the back. Pats on the back are okay, but do not become dependent on them. Remember that ego inflation is a feeling and you are learning to live beyond feelings. So when you do well and need recognition recognize it and feel good for you. Feel good because of who you are and who you are becoming, not because of deeds, as remember you have learned to separate, recognize and respect the person beyond the deed.

(Day 34) 3.5 Living beyond your feelings

Now is the time to take control of your mind and life by accepting responsibility for your decisions and feelings. It is time to put away all the imaginary thinking and move beyond any ego strongholds that may be affecting your decision making processes and happiness. The time for ego satisfactions is over and you have already been learning to live beyond these feelings, while continuing through recovery and your new ways of looking at life and all the good that it has to offer to those willing to find the courage to take some chances, while making some good changes.

Remember that most of life is lived in your thoughts and many of these thoughts are from feelings that you can take control of, so that you can have greater control of your true recovery life. In moving forward you need to remain open to new questions, while staying prepared to discover new truths about you and your life as it is time to make the responsible decision to find the real truths that you will need to advance your C.P.R. recovery life.

You will start today by remembering that you are as much a person and have as many rights as anyone and that you can be healed through your good decision making. It will be through your hard work and decisions that your life will be changed, with the only limits on your new life being the ones that you allowed in your way. You harness the power of change and of a better life through your reasoning and your decision making ability and it is past time to start putting this power into action by accepting responsibility and taking control of your feelings.

You will see that you must make the decision to not live or judge yourself by how, or what, you are feeling, at any moment in time. You will also find that you can be in control of your life without having the feelings of being in control, as you learn to quit living by these feelings; because trying to base life on feelings, is the kind of living that you are eliminating.

Now is the time that you must learn to live beyond your thoughts and beyond your feelings and to learn to be the person that you are becoming, not the person that once you were, or that others think you to be.

You have the ability to change and to enjoy life, starting right now, no matter what your feelings and thoughts say, so decide to be happy for what you are capable of becoming and do not live moment to moment, or day to day, any longer; when you can live decision to decision and decide right now that you are going to make good decisions and that you are going to be okay.

Remember that everybody needs changes in life, so needing change should not be a factor in if you feel happy or worthy. This is a very simple and proven concept and yet people make it so hard for the mind to grasp, but you need to be different and you need to open up your mind and realize that your feelings belong to you, are specific to you and can be decided on and changed by you. They should not and do not need to rely on outside factors, so get ready to change them simply because you own them, they are yours and it is your decision to change and to be happy and you do not need anyone's permission for this.

Tell yourself and believe that you are happy and that you are becoming healthy in mind, body and spirit, while envisioning peacefulness, happiness and such, while repeating all the positive self affirmations you can think of through your day.

Take this down and know it as truth, you do not have to feel something to be something, as you are not what you feel, you are what you make yourself to be. Remember that it is a new hour, with new decisions and it is time to break old traditional feelings and false beliefs. You must learn that you not only have the right to do and feel good today, but that you are also the vehicle of change that is going to bring about the change and the best that there can be in your life, because no matter how bad you think that you may be, you can be and can do better, starting by understanding how your feelings influence your actions, or reactions, through daily life.

Remember, a feeling is just a receptor in your body that gives you something to think about, but that does not make it true or false, or real or fantasy, or good or bad at least not until you finish the equation by you adding your personal interpretation leading into your response.

(Day 34b) **3.5 #1 study thought. Living beyond your feelings**

Tell yourself and believe that you can, will and are becoming healthy in mind, body and spirit, also envision the positive visualizations of peace and happiness, while repeating all the positive self affirmations that you can find for yourself, as it is time to fully realize that you do not have to feel something to be something, as you are not what you feel and you are not what someone else feels, or supposedly makes you feel.
This should be a simple concept, but often it is not, yet it is something that once you learn it you will know it and the changes in your life will last a lifetime and will make many typically difficult situations much easier to take care of.

To get started, answer a few questions for yourself, such as:
How many times have your feelings needlessly been hurt, by other's comments or thoughts? Often, never, daily?
Have you ever been made to feel bad, or like less of a person, by someone else, because of something that you did, or did not do? Have you ever been "made a fool of" or had your ego squashed by another who made fun of you or disgraced you?

These questions could go on forever, but the point is that we have all felt like we have been made to feel bad, seemingly by others, for certain things that have happened and the problem is that it is usually the feeling that is focused on, instead of on what truly matters, which is where the feeling comes from! What or who causes what you choose to feel? Who allows what you choose to feel? And who controls what you choose to feel?

Think about this; someone that you care about says terrible things about you and crushes your feelings, now before you fall into a ball of hurt feelings, stop for a moment and break this situation down. Someone you love has supposedly "hurt your feelings", or have you allowed your feelings to feel hurt? After all a feeling, is a thought inside you that you control! So this hurt is a thought from your ego. Your ego was hit and did its rounds in your thoughts and sent some results into your brain; so think about all that you are talking about here; your ego, your brain, your thoughts, your feelings, your pride, your decision to feel hurt and you should be able to recognize who is in control of how you decide to feel when someone says something, that you add your feelings to? Could you change how you decide to feel?

So what you have said is that you were hurt, as you allowed this, to allow your ego, to fill your feelings, which means that you allowed the hurt feeling, if you recognize it or not.
This also means that you control it; so you can accept it, deny it, change it or whatever you choose, as it just another person's legal right to their opinion, but this does not mean that you have to internalize it as they expect you to, so learn to live beyond it and leave it on the outside, as an opinion that reflects on the one giving it, not the one receiving it. It's just a piece of verbal mail and if someone hands you a letter that you do not want where do you file it, inside your mind or the trash?

Think about it, when words hurt your feelings, do you stay hurt forever, or get past it and move on, just because it is your decision to control your life and feelings. So now instead of just controlling the feelings that go out, you are controlling the feelings that come in. Do you give your power to others by allowing them to cause you self defeating hurt feelings, or do you recognize that it is your decision what your feelings do. There is not enough room to explain this fully, but you will get enough of an idea with the practice of controlling your feelings, that you will come to see the true power that you hold, by owning and retaining the power over your feelings.

Practice daily as you pay attention to things that once hurt your feelings and that you now control, by controlling the feelings, while realizing that you do not need to allow yourself to hold onto feelings of hurt, or pain, due to others trying to manipulate you, or cause you distress. Choose to use your power and time to feel good, instead of giving your power away to others who want you to feel bad. Right now in your thoughts and feelings start forgiving yourself and others for hurt feelings that your very own thoughts caused you to believe, as now you have learned to forgive and control your feelings, so choose to be content and then be content.

(Day 35) 3.5 #2 Living beyond your feelings

It is time to see that you must not live or judge yourself by how or what you are feeling. You are going to find that you can be in control of your life without having the feelings of being in control, as you learn to quit living by your feelings.

Now is the time for you live beyond your feelings and to become the person that you are becoming, not the person that you were, or feel like you are, or that others think you to be.

Think of all the false sayings that you have heard regarding feelings, that appear to be harmless talk and false comparisons; because they do say something about the way the brain works, as they are lies that play on feelings and no matter how you boil it down, when you are telling your mind things that are not true, than they are lies and when you feed your mind false illogical statements, then it may become confused, which means it could start believing that what it feels is real not realizing that it is only real because you believe it and not because it is true.

When choosing to feel something for the day, why not choose to feel confident, as confidence in oneself is a feeling and is a feeling that you have within you. Saying, I do not have any self confidence is just another choice and it is time to realize that the key to confidence is understanding that it is a feeling and remembering that with feelings that you can remain confident and in control, without feeling confident and in control and even though the feeling is nice, the confidence in oneself is necessary in eliminating negative feelings.

It is time to stop thinking that you need others approval to be confident. This is important as you already know what happens to self confidence when you spend time dwelling on negative consequences, it dwindles and becomes buried under senseless worry about others thoughts.

Once you learn to force your self confidence back into your conscious understanding, than you will be more likely to focus on the situation at hand, which will greatly enhance your positive productive confident life chances, as you gain a greater understanding of your chances, through your feelings of self control and the self control of your feelings.

Self control in itself is an art that consists of learning to be in control of emotions and feelings, while understanding that what you are controlling is feelings within yourself, these are feelings that you own and you choose how they will manifest in your daily life and there is a full range of thoughts, feelings and decisions to be decided by you, in how you will choose to feel, act and react at any given moment throughout a day.

So if you like it or not once you learn who has the power in your life it will come down to, if you want to feel happy then feel happy and if you do not want to be happy then don't be, but do not blame others for your decision, because just as you have the right to live life how you choose, so do they and they were not put here to make you happy and though they may influence your decision through their actions, it is still your decision to feel confident and in control or whatever you decide you want to feel.

Remember, a feeling is a receptor in the mind that you add your thoughts to, if you change the thought, you change the feeling. Think about how you are feeling right at this moment, now change it, right now, truly decide to feel different, preferably something positive e.g. choose to feel happy, until you just feel good, tell yourself a joke, think of a good memory, smile, sing, there are many things that you can do to change how you feel inside, just because it is your choice.

I have made a decision for myself that of everything the world can and has taken from me, it cannot take my happiness, because it is my feeling and my decision. This does not mean that I am always happy with the way things are, as I do not ever want to be complacent and I always want better, it means that I feel happy because I like the feelings associated with happy and it helps me to get much farther in life by keeping positive inside. So now even when I feel bad I realize that the bad is an outer layer that is temporary and I know that I still have happiness inside that is waiting to be expressed, once I relocate the burden that needs to be taken care of, whatever it may be.

You have got to choose how you are going to feel and react to everything that happens every day and if you learn to get beyond negative reactions, through positive actions, than your life will become much more manageable.

(Day 35b) 3.5 #2 study thought. Living beyond your feelings

How many things can you think of, in relation to your true feelings, that you have lied to yourself about; maybe not meaning any harm, just harmless chatter, not even what some would consider a lie, as it is just a saying, but stop and think about what your "just talk", or sayings, are really saying and when it comes right down to it, is it the truth, or a lie?

While retraining your brain you have to be careful about the things that you are saying. Remember that your mind has been conned into believing many things throughout addiction and now you need to stick with factual truths, as you weed the garbage feelings out. e.g. I felt like the world was against me.

Feelings often pertain to false threats, perceived through the ego, which you do not need to feel, such as when people disagree with you, others can disagree with you without you feeling threatened if you change the feeling. Change your thoughts, change your rationalization and change the feeling. Remember a feeling, or ego threat is nothing more than a thought or word, so take the thoughts away from the feeling and the feeling away from the thoughts and spend some time thinking on the positive things that you could choose to feel.

Granted it is hard to think on the good life, when you are feeling bad, but like some jobs life can be hard, but when you have a job to do, if you want to reach your goal, you do the job, hard or not, so now your job, hard or not, is to concentrate on the good, the good in you, in others, in life, in your mind, even when life is tough.

If you want to feel better, than it is your job to feel better and no one else can do it for you. You have to change yourself, your talk, your thoughts, your feelings, your attitude and your life as you work for change through your decision making process.

Take control of and change the thoughts that you give to the feelings and instead of telling yourself how bad, sad and lonely that you feel, recognize that you may feel a little down and tell yourself that you do not have to feel bad for that and then do not waste anymore time feeling negative when you can be concentrating on feeling whatever you choose to feel.

Choose to feel different just because you can, remember you do not have to have wonderful things going on in your outer world to be happy in your inner world, find your own true inner peace, and quit wasting energy on trying to change the world, when you only need to change a part, so change the part that you can and then you have changed the world.

You have the right to your feelings and you have the right to, control them, change them and express them, to your benefit, so start deciding to make the most positive experience for yourself that you can and you will see positive change.

You get to choose how you are going to react to and feel about the things that happen in your every day and in your life.

Think about some of your feelings; hurt, anger, disgust, thirst, need, fear etc. What kinds of things do you think on when you have these feelings, where do you actually feel these feelings? Are they felt in your mind and if so and you made up your mind to not feel them, what would happen to the feeling?

How do you feel about retraining your thoughts, so that feelings and emotions would not be able take control of your thinking, as it would become your decision what you spent your valuable time thinking on?

Remember that you are not looking to dismiss your feelings, but to fully understand and deal with them without allowing them to be controlled by your emotions. It is also time to stop creating feelings based on these emotions, that in turn effect your choice of actions or reactions based upon the emotions and feelings, because as you change your interpretation of the emotion and feeling, than you will have a chance to change the response and in effect your daily life.

4.0 Preparing for action

Life changing decisions are coming your way and you cannot avoid them, but you can use them to positively affect your day, as every minute holds a decision of power that may just lead you towards the life that you are seeking, but if you are not mindful it could also send you spiraling out of control; as every decision has the potential to be good or bad, to make you happy or sad, or a number of other things and it is up to you how you will deal with your decisions and responses. Your decisions are your responsibility and you are going to have to make some good choices while remembering that even choosing to not do anything, or to not take responsibility, is a decision and is your responsibility, even if it is a decision to be irresponsible.

Every decision that you have ever made, or decided to not make, has affected your life, maybe in ways that you do not realize or see, but change is change and it is time to accept responsibility and to keep making good decisions for your life.

Now all decisions are not going to be easy, they are not supposed to be and all decisions are not going to make your life better, but in the long run, the good ones will and until then you can be happy knowing that you are doing what is right, even when it hurts, which shows maturity and growth. So use this growth to see how your decisions affect your life today, by reflecting on some of the hard decisions that you have made and the rewards or consequences from those decisions.

You must realize that self control in itself is the art of learning to be in control of emotions and desires, while understanding that what you are controlling is the feelings within yourself, which effect outer reactions, as these feelings that you choose to allow, do manifest into your daily actions.

Be assured that self control, like everything else, is learned through understanding, practice and being able to socialize it into your life. For example have you ever viewed someone else's demeanor and wished that you could be that calm, cool and collective; believe it or not you can, as you have the same thoughts and choices that they have and it is just time for you to stop and think and choose a different reaction than what you used to, as your reaction is a choice and you have the right to change your thoughts and to start being seen as the one who is in control, if you so choose to be.

You must practice and master self control, which will come through learning to keep thoughts and emotions in check while making a decision to not react on emotions. You must learn to wait until the emotion subsides, so that you can be sure to be acting through your control and not through quick temperedness.

Now is also the time to remain mindful and prepared and to stand against the distorted thinking from past negative behaviors as you remain armed with a positive decisive thought and productive action to combat against these thoughts and behaviors, which try to tempt and take hold of your thoughts, as you have realized that it is your responsibility to stop temptations from being turned into behaviors, by eliminating them completely, as even the thoughts from negative behaviors can distort your thinking.

So in working to avoid the tempting alcohol mindset you must stop hanging around where the temptations of negative talk and behaviors flow freely and you must stop condoning and making excuses for them. Keep breaking these bad traditions and ending bad decisions, as you keep learning that with some good decisions and faith that life and its battles can be won, one good decision at a time.

You must maintain this faith in yourself and believe that you can change and overcome through your ability to make good decisions for a better life and to have the courage to stand by those decisions, because without good decisions all the hoping in the world cannot manifest into a single thing to prepare you for the life changing decisions needed to keep your life moving forwards.

Now there may be setbacks, but through your decisions and faith you will be prepared and you will be able to persevere, as you take hold of and stand up to your responsibilities, which includes paying closer attention to your responses, as well as understanding your true abilities, as you become that person that you are becoming.

(Day 36) **4.1 Responses and abilities**

You are now working for a true responsibility towards self and others, as you remain mindful of the false responsibilities common among addiction thinking, including that which thinks that one can be a responsible drinker. Alcohol may be legal, but it is still just a drug of choice, which alters thought patterns and when a person is purposely and haphazardly altering brain chemicals with poison then they cannot rationally or logically be considered responsible.

It is time to realize that just because you eliminate some of the chances of a worse outcome and supposedly do no harm and even if you give it a pretty flavor and paint happy faces on it, alcohol is a poisonous substance, which changes brain activity and affects responses and abilities and can in no way be considered responsible by a logical responsible thinking person. This is where true maturity comes into play, because losing the; "well at least I did this or did not do that" is a hit to the minds rationalization process.

Now if you want to be responsible you can add; I made the decision to not use alcohol, because responsibility cannot be added to that which negatively affects and lowers your ability to respond properly, while doing damage to your mind, body, brain and nervous system.

The idea of responsible drinking of alcoholic beverages is a ploy to shift responsibility, as this drug causes chemical imbalances in the brain, causes thinking patterns to be disturbed affects the central nervous system and lowers inhibitions while changing thoughts, emotions, judgment and health. So how could someone say; be responsible using this stuff which makes it illegal, or dangerous, for you to do so many of the normal responsible activities of daily living; because your brain has been altered and you cannot be considered responsible, or safe, after altering your brains chemical balance with drugs and alcohol.

It is time to realize that responsibility is based on needs, not wants, as well as on what you do to make life better and safer, while doing what you should be doing; legally, morally and safely, when and where you should be doing it; to better yourself, your family and your community.

So you can spend your life justifying and making excuses for past poor decision making, or you can take responsibility and change your thoughts, as this is your power and it belongs with your good decisions, not with the excuses that you are willing to make for the past. You must remember that even though alcohol influences responses and abilities, you are still responsible for your actions, as you have the power to act on any thoughts that alcohol influences. So if you want to learn to be a better person than you have to break any influence that alcohol tries to bind to your mind.

Remember that alcohol, drugs and other things do not have true power, yet they can be given false ability by and through your thoughts, as you allow them to change your thinking, even as far as to have you say that they have power over you. You need to be cautious with this illogical and dangerous talk as your brain may come to believe that they do have power, or that you are a liar. So tell yourself the truth, which is that you hold the power, even if you do not use it properly, it is still your power, responsibility and decision and now is the time to make the right decision, to find the real truths and to learn to keep seeing things differently than past beliefs would have you see them.

Think about everything else you could be doing while your drinking and if there is not any place else that you could be, such as, with your family, kids, work, church etc, and nothing more constructive you could be doing with your family, kids, work, church etc, and nothing that needs done to better your relationship with your family, kids, work, church, community etc and if that time and money could not be used for the sake of your family, kids, work, church, or to help another etc., then maybe you really are where you are supposed to be at this moment in time, wasting time and money, altering your thoughts and damaging your body, your brain and your reputation? But even if you believe this is where you are supposed to be, this still does not equal responsible or logical and is a sure waste of your abilities and the time that you could be sharing with those who truly need you to be responsible, including yourself, so make a decision of responsibility, not just towards yourself, but towards your family and community as a whole.

(Day36b) 4.1#1 study thought. Responses and abilities

Give some thought to the following.
A. How do you view responsibility? How do you choose to use it? Remember that responsibility makes you accountable for you and is about making thought out logical responsible decisions in situations that require mature logical good thinking responses.

B. Responses are verbal or action packed replies that you have the ability to control, yet too often people forget to use the ability of thought before talk, which can cause disharmony, but you have the ability to admit that you spoke without thinking and you have the right to change your response and your decisions to fit the needs of the situation that you are facing.
Can you see where you need changes in how you respond to certain things? How will you change your ability to respond?

C. When you become quick tempered or judgmental, you are allowing others to use your power against you, as others can incite feelings in you that can change how you respond, but you have the ability to choose your responses and will be accountable for your reply. So make sure to remain in control and to keep your power, through your thought out responses.
How will you use your ability to control daily thoughts and decisions? Who has power over your responses and abilities?

D. Would you like others to view you as a responsible person? What does responsibility look like to you? There are things that you can do to make others look at you differently, you have already proven this, but more importantly than how others view you, is how you learn to view yourself.

E. What can you do to better your understand your true responsibilities? What are some things that you are already responsible for? How do you view and care for those things? What can you do to better fulfill those responsibilities?

What do you think about the following in regards to responsibility?

1. At least I do not drink and drive!
You must quit focusing on "the least" and realize that drinking and not driving does not make you responsible! Responsibility is not based on what you do not do. Drinking causes harm if you recognize it or not and drunk driving is dangerous and illegal; but you are responsible, for this irresponsible action and if you do not do it that is good, but that alone does not make you responsible; quit expecting pats on the ego, for doing less wrong than you could, as the lesser of two evils is still evil.

2. I only drink at home, to relax!
A lot of people only do drugs at home, or only abuse spouses and children at home, many harmful behaviors are only done at home, so what could only doing it at home tell you? Maybe that you are irresponsible and causing harm at home? So you see, you cannot win for losing, at least not with alcohol.

3. I use a designated driver.
A designated driver is a responsible idea, but it does not make you responsible. You can make good decisions and be irresponsible and it is time to stop trying to add I am a responsible drinker to your drinking just because you made a good decision. If you want to be responsible become the designated driver, not the designated drunk and again stop trying to make excuses in regards to alcohol and responsibility.

4. I only drink on occasion, or weekends, or special occasions.
This is a sad worn out excuse to try to convince yourself of your responsibility level. Well I could drink all the time, well yes you could and it is a good decision not to, but good decisions do not make you responsible; being responsible makes you responsible. Granted there are ways of acting responsible while drinking, with acting being the key word, as there may be good decisions and signs of knowing your limits, or not breaking the law, but they are not signs of responsibility. Responsibility has to do with doing what you need to be doing, when you need to be doing it.

(Day 37) **4.2 Do not just endure life, live it**

You can stand against and regain freedom from the wrath of past bad decisions, but you must recognize them for what they are, just past bad decisions and then follow through in the now, with new good decisions. Do not spend your day living in the wrath of the "what ifs" of the past, when you can be living in the now. You must regain control of and become master of your now, your thoughts and your life, as you find that life is not meant to be endured, especially in the past, it is meant to be lived, in the now, but you must stand up against negative thoughts, while making sure to use the proper tools to eliminate the negative strongholds tormenting your life.

Remember that much of life is lived in the thoughts, so do you choose to think that life is something that must be endured, or do you choose to view it as a series of events, with each 24 hour day being an event that you fill with activities.

To start living life and making it what you need it to be you must realize that you have not wasted life, as you are just learning how to live it. Past life was endured and has ended and new life is ready to be lived, so in your quest to get beyond enduring life, stop enduring the past, as you cannot live in the past and the present at the same time. Do not spend any more time enduring the wrath of something that you cannot change, when you can be spending your life living in the now. Even if past life events have made you feel sad, this does mean that life is sad, because you do not live by feelings, nor do you endure past hurts, you recognize them and deal with them in the now.

So now you will regain control of and become master of your mind, your thoughts and your life, as you would like to know them and this is when you find that life will be lived, not endured. Now you may have endured many life changing challenges and decisions, but that just shows that there are temptations waiting to do battle and though they should be avoided, sometimes people fall into these traps, but be assured that getting trapped is no reason to admit defeat, as this trap is just a thought and you do not have to endure it, as you can override feelings and move on with living new life.

In discovering new ways of looking at life you might look at your life decisions from an outside standpoint, take a step back and look at yourself from the outside in and be honest about the changes that you would like to see.

In your quest for this better life, you will find that there is a good life for those who seek it diligently, work for it wholeheartedly, believe in it unwaveringly and accept it unconditionally. You will also find that temptations, no matter how strong they may appear, can be overcome through responsibility, good attitudes, actions, strengths, perseverance and a decision to own, forgive and forget past decisions, as well as becoming responsible for present ones.

Negative downfalls and bad decisions that are part of life and that have affected your being can be overcome through good positive decision making efforts, which will in effect foster positive new life change, as life is meant to be lived positively and you are part of life, so it is time to put the past oppressive thinking away and make some new good decisions to start living life.

So you have 24 hours a day to live, or endure and to fill with activities and you get to choose how you view them, so start using this time to live a life where you are in charge of your feelings about all that happens in your 24 hour period. Choose your attitudes and thoughts well and remember again that much of life is lived in your thoughts, so choose them responsibly and start filling your day with good thoughts and your life will see positive change. These positive changes may not make life easier, but they will make life better and which would you rather have; as no matter how easy life becomes, if it was not going to be better in your own mind than what good would it be? Now even when life is harder, as long as you choose to feel better than it is good.

You need to take some time to think about your 24 hours of activity every day, as every person that makes it through today has filled and is starting another 24 hours with whatever attitude they chose to use; so start using your hours to live the life that you are in charge of, as it is solely up to you how you are going to view and what you are going to feel about your new day.

(Day 37b) **4.2 #1 study thought. Do not just endure life**

How do you view your daily activities? As work that has to be done? Do you make it a burden that you must endure? Or do you consider your job what it truly is, an activity that you get paid for and which helps fill the hours of the day. It does not matter if it is dealing with kids, school, work, or whatever you do every day, they are all just activities that fill the day and you can choose to view it, as positively or negatively, as you wish.

It may be hard to see everything you do as an activity, but give your mind a break and stop forcing a mindset of burden, when you can change your mindset and start living, by seeing that you are filling your days with activities that you will do your best at and be done with, until the new day starts again.

It is time to see that all the negative self talk, about how you may feel about something, before you even get to it, has a lot to do with how your day starts and ends and what you call your chores has a lot to do with if you live or endure life. Think of the things that people do to fill the hours of a day e.g. work, drive, cook, clean, drink etc. and think about the self talk and feelings that you feel and use with each, which describes how you feel when certain activities arise.

Think about how changing your talk from the drudgingly, somebody has to do it, just another day, I cannot stand it any longer, if I only had?, I am tired of being unappreciated, why am I the only one who?, I cannot do everything, I am just wore out; into a positive attitude of daily activities that you get to live for and be part of could change your whole days mindset to help with the activities that you are doing right now, as yesterdays are gone and tomorrows will be taken care of later, so stop living in all that you had to do yesterday and all you have to do tomorrow and just take care of today's activities.

Change how you talk about and feel about your day and your life will change. You can do this, because no matter how bad a job or day feels, it is just a feeling that you can change and control.

So along with your conscious decision to learn how to live life, you will need to practice some new ways to change the enduring life mindset, into one of fulfilling daily activities, while feeling good about your work, activity, day and life.

Life is about keeping an open mind and doing different activities better, to be able to better your life. Try this one, when you first wake up as well as during the day, clap your hands to get your attention and say out loud "this is a great day" and "I feel good today, because it is my decision to feel good" and then stop letting the outer world control your inner feeling of happiness, as it is truly your decision from within.

What about trying some simple things, like when someone asks you something about your life, job or day start paying attention to what you are saying and learn to keep it positive and productive. e.g. when asked how you are doing why say, I'm alive, I'm surviving, getting by, just another day; When you can say, hey I am feeling good and I mean it, this is a good day to be alive!, or even just "I feel good".

Stop talking to your mind like you are trying to convince yourself how hard it is be happy, when it is just a decision that you are making. Life may be hard; you may not have a choice about that, but the thoughts and feelings that you add are your choice, so pay attention and change them to fit new goals of living a new life.

When others are telling you how hard life is and how terrible people are, do not start agreeing, stop yourself, acknowledge their bad day, tell them that it is too bad that some things happen, but do not wrap yourself in their bedspreads of gossip or negativity.

Remember that you are now living positively, not enduring negativity, so do not endure others attempts to drag you into their self destructive thoughts about just enduring life and just getting by, when you can start living to the best of your ability.

(Day 38) **4.3 Talk the solution**

In continuing C.P.R. you will be working on self talk in relation to the solutions to the problems that may arise. Problems can be a normal part of life, but complaining about them only reinforces them and contrary to popular belief, talk is not cheap; as all of your negative talk burdens your conscious and unconscious mind. So now it is time to change your thinking and to realize that a problem is only a problem if you do not add a solution. Once you learn to bring solutions forward by learning how to think about the so called problems, then you will also find that there are actually fewer problems in life than what you believe. This becomes understandable once you start to realize how relative many issues actually are.

Many people live problem filled life's, by spending their days talking about what they do not have, what they cannot do, where they cannot go, or how they cannot this and that and the other. So pay attention to your talk and how often you talk about problems that you think you have, or how much you talk about others problems and you may just find that some people have been socialized to spend time in negative self talk, while focusing on what they do not have and cannot do, instead of talking about all that they can do and all that they do have.

It is time to realize that if you spend your life talking about problems than you are keeping yourself in the "problems". It is time to leave these behind and start living in and for the solutions. You already have the solutions to any and all problems that could come your way and once you learn to realize that, you will become prepared to live a solution filled life, instead of just enduring a problem filled life.

A solution filled life says that you can handle things, because of being pre-pared or pre ready; ready in advance, for what may come your way; it is living with a responsible insight, foresight and knowledge of life, the self and of your possible behavior and attitude choices, which pertains to your responses and abilities and comes through practicing and working your C.P.R. recovery, while understanding and believing that there is always a better way to act, in every situation.

So you already have the solutions to the problems that could come your way and once you learn to realize this, you will become better prepared to live a solution filled life, as you start realizing that there are no real problems, only situations seeking solutions, so become solution oriented and be prepared to stay in control of your thoughts, feelings and emotions and there is nothing that can come your way that you cannot walk through victoriously. To learn these better, you will continue changing your thinking, by continuing to use your positive aggressive "I will" statements that turn the once thought about problems, into positive oriented obtainable solutions, so change the wording and turn the problem into an obtainable or workable goal.

It is time to see that so called problems are a natural part of life and when you think about how logical most of life is not, then it becomes more understandable that it would be odd if there were not pitfalls, as most situations have built in issues waiting to be dealt with, but as long as you are prepared, than you will be able to counter any problems, with good positive thoughts and behaviors.

As you are becoming solution oriented, you will need to learn to take this positive talk with you throughout your day. So again remember that it is time to realize that if you spend your life talking about problems, than you are keeping yourself in the problems and it is time to leave these behind and start living in and for the solutions, as you already have all the solutions to all the problems that could come your way and once you learn to realize this, you will become prepared to live a solution filled life, instead of just enduring a problem filled life.

Also remember that a solution filled life says that you can handle all things, due to your living with a responsible insight of those things that your mind once considered troublesome, as well as understanding that those problems are just issues that you have not added your solution to yet, as you have learned to consciously weigh out the possible behavior and attitude choices, as well as deciding on your most responsible responses to the situation before acting on it and possibly causing a problem, instead of a solution.

(Day 38b) **4.3 #1 study thought. Talk the solution**

Think about where problems seem to pop up in your life and you will likely see that many situations have built in issues to be dealt with, but as long as you remain armed and ready with built in productive solutions, than you should be able to counter these with logical solutions, or at the least with some good positive thoughts.

Think about the advantages of being prepared and solution oriented and how beneficial it would be to be able to be internally prepared. In other words what is the benefit of having the proper tools ready, not to live in fear, but to live in the power of preparedness, so as to say that you are prepared with a solution if need be.

Try to think of some things in life that may model solution oriented thinking and preparedness. Start out with some simple examples; remembering that the object is just preparing your mind to understand the benefits of solution oriented thinking.

Why do cars come with a spare tire? So that if you get a flat, not a problem, you are prepared, with a positive solution! Why do cars have oil and other gauges? If the oil gets low, no problem, you are prepared. Why do houses come with locks on the doors, circuit breakers on wiring, why are there stop lights, a 911 emergency service, why do we teach children so many safety issues, or life issues etc.

You can ask and answer these same questions in relation to any negative behaviors, as you have the right to and should question things that affect your life. e.g. Why do some programs say that you cannot quit using on your own, which you can fix this by saying not a problem, unless I buy into their theory, but I can say no to programs that would require my beliefs in things that may be harmful to my conscious and/ or unconscious mind and yet that do not come with a positive productive solution, because I am prepared with a solution, for those things that I allow into my life.

Think about problems that you have, or expect, or which you have not dealt with and allow to take up space in your mind.

For a starter do you see any of the following as problems in your life; I drink or smoke too much, I need a better place to?, I do not have enough ?, my back aches, my car needs fixed, people do not understand me, I am afraid, I feel like ?, I need ?, I can't ?, etc.

Which items on your list are problems that need fixed, which are conditions that need changed and which need dismissed as just facts of life? Be careful not to dismiss those which you <u>feel</u> that you cannot deal with, only those that you truly cannot change!

All problems have solutions, some you have to think about, but by becoming solution oriented and learning to prioritize and prepare for life solutions, you will find that it is only a problem if you cannot do anything about it and it affects your life directly and then it's only a problem if you do not let it go.

Take all of your "I wish, I want, I need" or "I cant's" and replace them with the positive aggressive "I will" statements that will give you a positive obtainable goal towards ending the problem. e.g. Change I drink too much, into, not a problem I will quit drinking! Somebody does not like or talked about me, not a problem; I will respect their opinion and not let it bother me. Go over your list of "problems" and add your solution oriented thinking e.g. "it's not a problem, as I will?" and add your solution.

You are the master of true change in your life even though you cannot control changes in the world; you can control changes in your world, through working on your positive life solutions.

It is time to start living with a responsible insight and knowledge of one's behavior choices, which pertain to responses and comes through practicing and working the C.P.R. plans and understanding and believing that there is always a better way to act and do, in every situation.

(Day 39) **4.4 Insight, faith and truth**

In preparing for recovery you will learn that the truth does not always have to make you happy or be awe inspiring, but it does have to make you think about positive change and life as it guides you to reach deep within yourself, to answer truths about yourself that you will need to carry you forward through recovery.

You will be guided by insight and faith, as well as absolute and relative truths. These relative truths are statements or observations that contain some extent of truth. This could be something that you know as truth, which has not been proven as absolute, just the truth as some know or believe, which again could be the truth, but without proof it is still relative, or truth as I hear it, whereas absolute truth is proven to be factual. If you are a compulsive drinker, than the real truth is that you have a behavioral condition and the absolute truth is that you are a person and no matter how hard of a choice it is, you can choose not to drink.

It is going to take your full thought and ability to get in touch with and understand your true insight, as you have the ability to view situations clearer than what you believe and it is time to start trusting your perception of the situations that are affecting your life.

Insight offers a good tool of awareness for understanding situations, as insight builds on faith and breeds inspiration. This faith which is growing through your new found insight and inspirations is the confident belief and trust in oneself, as a person. This is a powerful tool in your recovery, as faith works on a different kind of power and inspiration and is not based on proven truth; it is based on positive good truths as you know them in your inner being. The thing that sets this apart from relative truths is that faith will never cause you to harm another, as it works in the realm of what is good and true.

I know that C.P.R. is going to touch lives that need to be touched. I know this as true through faith. Faith is described as a belief in that which is not seen; believing by trusting, while understanding through insight and inspiration. Faith is also one of those things that the more you use it the stronger it gets, so do not be shy in putting it to work for you, always keep your faith and it will always keep you.

This faith which is growing through your new found insight is the confident belief and trust in the truth, as well as a newfound faith in oneself, as a good and vital person. This faith, though built on relative truths, will prove to be a powerful and vital tool in your recovery, as it works on a different kind of power and inspiration and is based on positive good truths, that you know in your heart to be true. The main thing that sets this apart from relative truths is that faith will not cause harm, as it works on love, truth and happiness and is based on what is good and true, whereas a relative truth can contain harmful thoughts.

Faith contains the positive uplifting ideals, beliefs and truths to guide ones thoughts and behaviors into a greater understanding of life and oneself.

Most everything you know started as faith, by believing what you were taught from parents, teachers, adults, so to have faith is to believe or trust in something, that you believe to hold a good probability of truth, with no guarantee, as even though truth can build faith, faith cannot build truth; though it can build stronger faith and beliefs in one's personal abilities and can be a great tool when used properly, with the key being that you have to use it and work it, because just like every other tool that you own, faith does not do any good on its own, or by just having it.

You should come to realize that relative truths are statements that may contain some extent of truth, but relativity means changing, which means this "truth" can change as circumstances change.

What "truths" can you think of in your life that you have not proven as true, but were told or assumed them to be truth and how would you classify them, remembering that absolute truth is empirically proven truths, but be careful with absolutes, as most things are interdependent with or dependent on other circumstances which are changing, also remember that relative truths may or may not be true, as they too are dependent on things staying the same, when they are capable of change.

(Day 39b) 4.4 #1 study thought. Insight, faith and truths

To understand faith, think about the following and you may find that you use more than you think.

A. Do you know what day you were born and how old you are? How do you know you were told the truth? How do you know the birth certificate is real? Because that's what you were told and believe, that is fine, but call it what it is, it is a statement of faith; in basic common form, but still faith.

B. After working at your job you expect to get paid, do you get paid or do the work first, with faith that you will get paid.

C. When you go to the store do you have faith that they will have what you need, this is an expectation of faith.

D. I have faith that my child will be passing to the next grade.
E. I will quit drinking someday can be a statement of faith.

F. I know that God exists and that He loves us, flaws and all and that He will work with you through your faith.

G. I have complete faith that you can find your good decision making abilities and change your life into a sea of good decisions and I have faith that you can to turn this into truth.

Some of these may be irrelevant, but they are faith, so think about all the things that you do and deal with where you use daily faith and start concentrating on where true faith lies.

Think of those things that can become truth, through a willingness to believe, such as your statements of faith.

I know that all that the good life has to offer is waiting for me.
Be assured that material life and the good life are not the same, so if you are seeking happiness, quit looking to the material world, as having everything would not give you the good life.

I know that you can eliminate alcohol from your life and become the person that you would like to, as it is true that you have the ability to quit drinking, even if you do not see it yet.

This faith that you use every day, affects your whole life; through your thoughts and beliefs, so keep this powerful tool working for you, exercise it by using it, pay attention to it and understand it, do not be shy or afraid of it as you start telling yourself "I have faith in me", "I know that I can be better" etc.

How do you see yourself taking control of and using your faith, insight, absolute and relative truths in your recovery life?

Give some examples of each and study them to make sure they are set for you to get the most out of each.

What does insight mean to you?
How does it pertain to your now life?
How will you use it to benefit your recovery life?
What can you do to ensure that you get the most out of it?

What does faith mean to you?
How does it pertain to your now life?
How will you use it to benefit your recovery life?
What can you do to ensure that you get the most out of it?

What does truth mean to you?
How does it pertain to your now life?
How will you use it to benefit your recovery life?
What can you do to ensure that you get the most out of it?

What does relative truth mean to you?
How does it pertain to your now life?
How will you use it to benefit your recovery life?
What can you do to ensure that you get the most out of it?

What does absolutes and absolute truths mean to you?
How does it pertain to your now life?
How will you use it to benefit your recovery life?
What can you do to ensure that you get the most out of it?

(Day 40) **4.5 Decisive superiority**

Life decisions are always coming and they are your responsibility and you are going to have to make some real choices as to what to do about them. So it is time to become more decisive in your decision making, as you need to respect this ability to make conclusive decisions about your life. This is the time to stand firm in what you intend on accomplishing, as your life needs no indecisive areas, as you need to be operating on yes I can do this. Decisive superiority says that you will take the responsibility and the time to make superior decisions by making decisions based on facts and truths and to the best of you ability, to affect your life in the most positive productive manner possible.

You need to realize that it is not the talk, nor the walk, that will get you to where you are seeking to be, but is the combination of all your resources and abilities, tied together to be used by you in the most superior way possible through your good decisions. You will find that positive self talk is the tool for your journey, but that without the walk your journey cannot move forward. The walk may be tough, but you have proven that you can walk through tough times and now you need to know that you can also walk through them victoriously. It is time for you to decide to do good for yourself, not one week, day, or even hour at a time, but one good decision at a time and before long you will find yourself making groups of good superior decisions.

With your new decisions you are changing more than just your mind, decisions and bad habits, but also your way of life and now that you have the capacity for rational logical thinking, you know that you can manage life through superior decisions, because it is your decision and your goal to do so.

It is time for unquestionable decisive superiority which comes through unmistakable good decisions in your life in regards to all that you think and believe and all that you find to be good and true.

It is also time to look at those times when you felt as though you were buried beneath more than you could handle, when in actuality you were just like an oak tree seed, covered up with tons of dirt, but only buried if it decided to lay there and die, as seeds of life are not buried, they are planted, with the potential for full growth if one decides to push its way through the sludge and shake the dirt off to become firmly grounded, while reaching towards full life growth.

So ask yourself, if that simple little planted seed became a great towering mighty oak or a beautiful and elegant spreading maple, showering life with all its magnificent beauty and awe and you cut off its water supply and started feeding it life and oxygen depleting alcohol and drugs, what would happen to that strong beautiful mighty creation, that had been firmly grounded in true life? It would wither, become weak, lose its will and die, as would any living creature, including you, because when you feed on poison, your mind, life, hopes and dreams become intoxicated, only to wither and die.

The good news is that just as a seed is not buried, so goes it with the individual battling behavior conditions, you are not buried and if you feel that you are than you must live beyond the feelings. You must make the decision to change your thinking and realize that you are planted in life and it is time to start growing towards your full potential by looking in the right direction and reaching for the top, while pushing your way through the dirt, grime and sludge that you have allowed to settle on top of your branches.

So stop reaching for battles with bottles of alcohol, or pills and start reaching for life's possibilities to get you beyond any self imposed oppressions, because even if you never reach the top, the higher you reach and the more dirt you shake off along the way, the stronger you will stand in your new life.

You have power and you are not at the end of the rope, you are at the beginning of new life and it is time to learn that when life's drama's enter your space, that you have a decision to make; either to push them away and trust and grow in faith, or to partake in these traps and watch life wither and possibly die. Always remember that life's hardships and downfalls have the possibility of moving you in one of two directions, you can decide to let them land on your ego and push you down, or you can transfer them to your good thinking spirit of well being and deal with them, maturely and properly, as you put them beneath you, not behind you to nag you, but beneath you, so that you can use them as building blocks to stand above that which would otherwise wish to tear you down.

Hard times can be used as chances for growth and life is about growth, so start building past those things that would otherwise tear you down. Get out of the ego mode and do not live by, or let your ego run or ruin your life or it may be become a very unfulfilling life of being pressed down to the ground. Let your spirit of well being take over that which comes your way and start reaching and towering over the life that awaits you with the power and spirit of your sober minded good decision living.

Now is the time to learn to move through and beyond life's dramas and to trust in new growth and to help with this you will need to understand how growth works. Always remember that life's downfalls have the possibility of blocking out the light and hindering true growth, through your lack of understanding that true hardship is caused from the negative interpretation of feelings and that you can grow above any of these oppressive hardships by changing the feelings and leaving them behind, as you grow and rise above them, while taking responsibility and understanding that feeling buried, is not buried, it is a feeling that you planted in your mind.

In order to understand this fully you need to be able to understand what constitutes a seed in your life. A seed is something that you plant, which can grow into something bigger; sometimes good, sometimes bad and usually dependent on how you take care of it.

This is where you need to learn to think outside of the norm, as a lot of what you are going to be planting and bringing forth in your life is thoughts, attitudes, ideas and feelings and you need to learn to plant these seeds, e.g. thoughts, attitudes, ideas and feelings, into the proper places within yourself, your mind and your life as well as within others thoughts and minds which may also affect your life and your full recovery.

(Day 40b) 4.5 #1 study thought. Decisive superiority

Before you continue planting seeds in your life, you need to be sure that you have fully made the decision to forgive the past? If not, do it now and remember that when you make a decision, that you must put action behind it, or it is just talk.

Have you made the decision to stop listening to and letting others make decisions about you and your life?
What other things have you made the decision to do and change in your thinking and life?

Through decisive superiority you are going to learn the self discipline which you will use to build your confidence, as you learn to deny the negative self satisfactions of bad thinking.
You will show that you have what it takes to build this confidence in yourself through your understanding that you are capable of superior self control, through personal thoughts and decisions.

Think about the confidences that you are willing to plant in yourself and bring forth in your life, while remembering that if you tell your mind something enough times, it will come to believe it and if it is a productive truth than it may help you to learn to live life to your full potential.

So start planting while thinking about positive thoughts, ideas and decisions and start repeating, believing and socializing these into your new superior thinking, because if you want it to work, than you must work it.
Try the following to get started; I am confident and I know that I can successfully work this plan, because it is my decision to do so. I know that I am becoming stronger every day and will continue to through my confidences and will not allow others negativity to drag me down. I am confident that my life is getting better every day and will continue to get better, decision by decision, as I have the confidence and the solutions to carry me through new life victoriously. I am confident that I am going to retain control of my life and my good decision making processes, as I remain confident about being confident.

(Day 40c) **4.5 #2 Study thought. A time to plant.**

Now that you have some confidences in your abilities this is a good chance to be able to understand life ideas, while learning to use your imagination and creative thought to build on some new life ideals.

Remember that much of life is lived in the mind, so it is time to use your imagination to look towards greater possibilities through positive thinking tasks. For this new task, your imagination is going to come in to play, while thinking about true life growth. To understand this growth you are going to plant some new seeds, while also understanding some past ones, which will come by seeing what a seed may go through to get to its most mature state. So look out your window and pick a tree, or find one in your mind and study on it, what kind is it, how big, how many branches, what color leaves, how long has it been there, what has it been through and seen, does it serve a purpose? Now remove it in your mind, as it is time to understand what it went through to get to where it is, so you are going to step back in time and plant it and watch it as it grows and remember that sometimes it takes thinking about and seeing things differently to learn new ways of viewing or living life.

So this fragile little seed is going to learn to live and endure life after it is stomped underneath a world of dirt and darkness, of which it could just lay there and die just as any living thing could, or it could realize that it is planted and just like you, when something is planted, it is because it is alive and has potential and can choose to reach forward, onward and upward, or can choose to lay there and rot.
So the seed starts growing and reaching through the darkness, aiming for the sky and it will remain in control, as long as it does not give into the hard times and tough feelings that are coming its way. There will be animals trying to kill or eat it; kids who pick at it, climb it, break it down or mow it over, weeds trying to strangle it, insects infesting it, disease rotting it and the weather trying to drowned it, starve it, freeze it, burn it up, blow it down, rip it to shreds and so on, all through its life.

Take a moment to look around and think about how every living plant, animal and person alike has come from a fragile seed that has faced many life pitfalls and yet has kept pushing forward, because that is what life is and what living things do, they strive to be the best that they can, with what they have.

So with all that this tree has endured it keeps living, striving and reaching for the sun, even though it can never reach it. So why does it keep reaching? Can it grow beyond all the oppression and become strong and firmly rooted by its own power? Could it be that the direction of growth and reaching towards a goal is more important than the final destination, or even achieving the goal?

So now is the time for you to start a new season of planting, while understanding your true life goals.

A. What kind of seeds will you plant e.g. seeds of happiness, hope, friendship, responsibility, sadness, fear, anger? What new things are you willing to plant and grow in your new life?

B. Where will you plant these seeds? In yourself, others, minds, hearts? e.g. I will plant a seed of happiness in my heart, as well as a seed of responsibility towards myself; I will plant a seed of love within my child and forgiveness within my spouse etc.

C. How will you plant these seeds of hope, love, trust, etc., which are planted in minds via thoughts, words and actions.

D. How will you feed and grow your seeds, as they cannot just be planted and left, they need nurturing or they will die, but if they are nurtured properly than they will grow, as will you.

E. Once you have planted seeds of hope, responsibility, love and all that you have planted, like all planted life; it can be destroyed if not treated mindfully. You now must keep these seeds vitalized by continuing on with positive productive thoughts, attitudes and actions. Do not become discouraged, start planting and seeding and nurturing, as you need to get as many good thoughts growing as you can and though they may not all grow, keep them good, so that the ones that do not grow on the first planting, can be replanted.

5.0 Stronger than life's storms

Never close your eyes on your dreams, as they are just beginning with your new C.P.R. values, which started as your recovery stronghold, and now has become your life stronghold. Remember that it matters not, what others feel that you can, or cannot accomplish, as you have found the power of full recovery and a full satisfying sober thinking good decision making life and now all that you have to do is the best possible job that you can do, while accepting and taking responsibility for your decisions, actions and your life.

Be sure to keep striving for change, knowing that change is not a place that you reach and does not happen in a day, a week, or a year, it happens over a lifetime with each and every decision, of every day and it needs to be maintained as such, as you continue forward with continuous positive growth.

So again full recovery is not about where you end up, it is about where you are facing and about keeping moving in the right direction, while being mindful of how you act and react along the way. Be sure to stay focused on becoming that which you are becoming; which is a sober, responsible, viable human being, that has learned to live up to your own standards and responsibilities.

Remember also that the world does not have to be happy for you to be able to feel and be happy. You will choose to feel happy, because of who you are and who you are becoming, as this is a feeling that is about you and one that you get to choose. You can choose to feel happy, no matter what is happening outside, as all of the feelings that are within you gain power from and through your thoughts; so take this job of deciding your feelings very seriously, as you continue on with living your C.P.R. life, one good decision at a time.

Now you have a head start on life and can start back at the beginning of C.P.R., or whatever C.P.R. plan you would like to study deeper, while working your way through your next 6 week C.P.R. activity session, remembering that true learning and socialization, just like the good life, requires repetition of good thoughts so do not waste time; start repeating your daily plans and activities today, while maintaining your sober thinking for right now.

Welcome to your new BEGINNING

Now is your chance to be a blessing to another

If you know someone whose life could be healed, helped or changed through Comeback Power Recovery then now is your chance to be a bigger part of the solution and a world changer by making the decision to get copies of C.P.R into those hands that are in need of true life change and personal self recovery.

In becoming united towards a better and sobering way of life, think about this; with you and me standing together for positive change, that would double the number of people in our group and if we doubled that every day, there would be four of us tomorrow, then eight, sixteen, etc. keep doubling that every day with the help of those joining in and in 30 days we would have 10 million people working to be better people and that is true exponential growth and as unfeasible as it sounds it is possible, as each person, each day, would just have to recruit one new person, which means that you only need to recruit 30 people and each of them would each end up recruiting between one to 30 people, at one per day, to be able to reach 10 million people and that is factual truth. Now we may not be able to double our numbers every day, but working together we can share and bring recovery and a better way of life to those seeking to find a better way and with a little insight, love, preparation and action, along with a lot of good positive understanding and decisions, we can bring about positive change in many lives, including our own; one person and one decision at a time.

The Beginning

Clean and sober

Comeback Power
Recovery
(C.P.R.)

Self Recovery
from
alcohol, drugs
and
negative behaviors.

A true gift of love and hope

www.ingramcontent.com/pod-product-compliance
Lightning Source LLC
Chambersburg PA
CBHW060038040426
42331CB00032B/1033